KU-776-640

UNIVERSITY OF
GLASGOW

The Love Drug
Marching to the Beat of Ecstasy

Pre-publication
REVIEWS,
COMMENTARIES,
EVALUATIONS . . .

"**E**cstasy (MDMA) is a mixed stimulant and hallucinogen used since the mid-80s at acid house parties and raves. Cohen does an admirable job of explaining for the several million E or X pill users who may be hoping to find 'love' what their chances of avoiding death, hyperthermia, lethargy, convulsions, hepatitis, memory loss, panic, depression, and a host of other X-related mental disorders might be. MDMA may be used for euphoria or pleasure or to facilitate social interaction but avoiding the depression, paranoia, and irritability during acute abstinence and the memory and other major medical consequences may not be so easy. The title *The Love Drug: Marching to the Beat of Ecstasy* may make it sound like a popular book but it is a well-referenced and scholarly review for health professionals."

Dr. Mark S. Gold
Brain Institute,
University of Florida,
Gainesville

The Haworth Medical Press
An Imprint of The Haworth Press, Inc.

The Love Drug
Marching to the Beat of Ecstasy

The Love Drug
Marching to the Beat of Ecstasy

Richard S. Cohen

The Haworth Medical Press
An Imprint of The Haworth Press, Inc.

Published by

The Haworth Medical Press, an imprint of The Haworth Press, Inc., 10 Alice Street, Binghamton, NY 13904-1580

DISCLAIMER

Medicine is an ever-changing science. As new research and clinical experience broaden our knowledge, changes in treatment and drug therapy are required. While many suggestions for drug usages are made herein, the book is intended for educational purposes only, and the author, editor, and publisher do not accept liability in the event of negative consequences incurred as a result of information presented in this book. We do not claim that this information is necessarily accurate by the rigid, scientific standard applied for medical proof, and therefore make no warranty, expressed or implied, with respect to the material herein contained. Therefore the patient is urged to consult his or her own physician prior to following a course of treatment. The physician is urged to check the product information sheet included in the package of each drug he or she plans to administer to be certain the protocol followed is not in conflict with the manufacturer's inserts. When a discrepancy arises between these inserts and information in this book, the physician is encouraged to use his or her best professional judgement.

Cover design by Marylouise E. Doyle

Library of Congress Cataloging-in-Publication Data

Cohen, Richard S.
    The love drug : marching to the beat of ecstasy / Richard S. Cohen.
      p. cm.
    Includes bibliographical references and index.
    ISBN 0-7890-0454-2 (alk. paper)
    1. MDMA (Drug) I. Title.
RM666.M35C64 1998
615'.785—dc21

97-39231
CIP

CONTENTS

ABOUT THE AUTHOR

Richard S. Cohen, MA, is an independent researcher based out of central New Jersey. He has served on the editorial board of *Journal of Psychology and the Behavioral Sciences.* He is currently researching the effects of MDMA, or "Ecstasy." His previous studies pertaining to Ecstasy have been published in several scholarly journals, including *Progress in Neuro-Psychopharmacology and Biological Psychiatry,* as well as the official journal for the Society of Biological Psychiatry. Through his research related to prison populations, Richard Cohen co-authored an extensive review on Ganser's Syndrome resulting in a book chapter in *Explorations in Criminal Psychopathology* (Charles C Thomas). His most current research interests lie in the areas of substance use/abuse, anxiety-related disorders, depression, relationships, and issues pertaining to self-esteem.

Foreword

It was a Saturday night during the summer of 1991, and I was in New York City. I had gone out dancing before, many times in fact, but not in recent years. In the aftermath of my internship year, I found myself in a comfortable and exuberant place. But something was very different from other social gatherings. I had been on many dance floors in my life, while in college, at celebrations for my friends, in discos in the 1980s; however, people had never acted like this. Individuals were pumping, sweating, grinding, smiling, hugging, clapping, and surreally happy, yet obviously devoid of the kind of self-conscious behavior that I had associated with people dancing. I asked my dance partner, someone who knew this world far better than I, why people were acting in such an animated, yet benevolent manner. "Welcome to the world of Ecstasy" was the reply.

I had never heard much about Ecstasy, but I was impressed by the nature of this drug. Its ability to influence human behavior was profound and at the very least, fascinating. My original dance floor observations, as well as my follow-up research, indeed sparked my curiosity in exploring the facts behind this compound and the reasoning behind why people take Ecstasy.

Through extensive research, I was able to find out some basic truths about this unique substance. Ecstasy is actually the most popular nickname for 3,4-methylenedioxymethamphetamine (MDMA). I did not know until fairly recently that the compound is far from new and had actually been patented by a major company in the early 1900s. The original patent had been issued on Christmas Eve in 1914, thus prompting subsequent jokes for the next century from those who particularly loved the drug. There were even remarks sometimes made about the "best Christmas present ever."

Human consumption of Ecstasy is believed to have first taken place in the 1960s, a time of great experimentation among an entire host of people. There has been little solid data about early recreational use of this drug. The use of MDMA, perhaps more than any other drug, is influenced by its set and setting. This compound has been used by two distinct groups. Although the dichotomy is artificial, it is useful in the overall understanding of this drug. One group had used Ecstasy as a kind of tool for a therapeutic or spiritual journey. The other group had used and continues to use this substance for strictly recreational purposes. The split between the spiritualists and the partiers exists to this day.

With the widespread usage of Ecstasy and vast media intervention in the 1980s, especially in Texas, the legal manufacture and use of this compound was brought to an abrupt halt. Although the bureaucratic maneuvering of the scheduling of this drug remains highly controversial, the use and sale of MDMA have been illegal since that time. An unfortunate consequence of being banned and placed as a Schedule I drug, the most restrictive category, has been the near impossibility of further studying this alluring drug.

Much of the existing literature of MDMA is in the form of analytical reviews and individual case reports. The prompt prohibition of this substance resulted in a lack of solid, well-constructed, and implemented medical data available for compilation. Because of the hysteria and irrationality surrounding drug use in this country, and the drug's Schedule I status, it has been virtually impossible to study Ecstasy and its effects on humans. Therefore, many unanswered questions remain.

What is well known, however, is that MDMA is a powerful and intriguing compound. Most individuals who have ever taken the drug will happily attest to this. Ecstasy has profound and vividly memorable effects on its users. There are dangers associated with the drug, and although such anomalies are not completely understood, they may possibly be severe and permanent.

Richard S. Cohen has carefully composed a remarkable book on this increasingly popular, yet often misunderstood substance. *The Love Drug* is presented in a methodical manner, thoroughly covering the history of this compound, its pharmacological activity, and its emergence and ongoing surge upon the recreational domain—including its use at the ever so popular rave parties. Denizens of the rave scene, professional communities, and other curious and enticed readers will learn a vast amount of knowledge about Ecstasy upon reading this book and better understand what it actually is that one is either ingesting or considering ingesting.

David M. McDowell, MD

Preface

Throughout this past decade, a great deal of confusion has emerged with regard to the substance that has become infamously known by its nickname, "Ecstasy." A considerable amount of perplexity exists surrounding the history of this substance, the proper classification for this drug, and the overall scope of the effects that this substance induces.

In this book, Richard S. Cohen provides his readers with a multipurpose and convenient source for attaining an overall understanding of this mind-altering compound. He presents the information in a style that is appealing to individuals worldwide who are curious about, tempted by, and misinformed about the nature of Ecstasy and its diverse implications. Within this one text, readers are taken for a walk through every aspect of this drug. *The Love Drug* is educational, informative, and thought-provoking and provides answers to the most frequently asked questions about this substance.

Richard S. Cohen wrote this book in a well-balanced and broad manner foreseen as suitable for a wide range of individuals, from the novice browser to emergency room personnel. In a clear and concise manner, this book provides biochemists, physicians, pharmacologists, neurologists, psychiatrists, psychologists, social workers, lawyers, drug users, and everyday readers with a valuable reference source. For those readers wanting to save time from drawn-out literature searches, the references in this book provide a methodical track of the substance Ecstasy, with a plenitude of hard-to-find facts, all within one sitting.

James Cocores, MD

Author's Note

Regardless of whether you picked up a copy of *The Love Drug: Marching to the Beat of Ecstasy* for recreational reading or academic reference purposes, I believe this work will answer most, if not all, of your inquiries regarding Ecstasy. I have carefully composed this book in the most objective manner, with my goal being simply to inform. Although there are numerous technical Ecstasy-related articles in medical journals, there are relatively few sources available to the general public regarding this substance. Therefore, I have written this book in a manner that is detailed enough for educators, researchers, and clinicians, yet simple enough for the everyday reader.

This book is not drug-promoting material, and I certainly do not advise that anyone experiment with Ecstasy or any other substance available on the underground drug market. This book will, however, enable you to follow the history of Ecstasy from its initial patent to its present-day use as a recreational substance. After reading this text, you should have a better understanding of what has the nightlife crowd in Tokyo, New York, and London raving while medical professionals and civic officials the world over are trying to raise a warning flag to a generation marching down the road of nonstop dancing, music, and ecstasy.

If you have any further questions, comments, or concerns after reading this book, please feel free to contact me at: Richard S. Cohen, c/o The Haworth Press, Inc., Book Division, 10 Alice Street, Binghamton, New York 13904-1580. I will make a point to respond to your letters and consider including some of your feedback and personal Ecstasy experiences in subsequent editions of this book.

Richard S. Cohen

Acknowledgments

I would like to take this opportunity to give credit where credit is undoubtedly due. There were many individuals who played either a direct or an indirect role in the successful completion of this entire project.

I am grateful to my family, Marty, Peggy, and Traci, for their ongoing patience, support, and unconditional love.

I extend my wholehearted appreciation to James Cocores, MD, to whom I shall be forever indebted.

I am grateful to David M. McDowell, MD, who spent numerous hours editing my work and providing subsequent feedback.

I gratefully acknowledge Alexander T. Shulgin, PhD, for his ongoing personal communications via letters and the telephone for the past several years. This work would not have been truly complete without the assistance of Dr. Shulgin.

I am appreciative of the many volunteers who willingly and anonymously spent the necessary time allowing me to interview them, thus broadening my knowledge of the Ecstasy experience and overall drug-induced state.

I thank Bill Cohen and Bill Palmer at The Haworth Press for their original and continued enthusiasm for this publication, and for providing me with this exciting opportunity.

I extend my wholehearted appreciation to Dr. Barry Stimmel, Donna Biesecker, Trish Brown, Karen Fisher, Dawn Krisko, Peg Marr, Paula Patton, Amy Rentner, Andy Roy, and Cookie Travis for their outstanding efforts and the role each of them played in editing, proofreading, revising, and formatting this work.

I am grateful to Marylouise Doyle for a wonderful and alluring cover design. Her creativity and imagination truly shines.

I extend my recognition and appreciation to Sandy Jones-Sickels, Matt Babcock, Margaret Tatich, Becky Miller-Baum, Christine Matthews, and the entire marketing and sales department at The Haworth Press. The marketing strategies for this book have been absolutely stellar.

I wish to acknowledge the assistance of Melissa Devendorf, who has been most helpful throughout the entire publication process.

Chapter 1

MDMA Is Born: Introducing Ecstasy

THE DRUG CRAZE

As we approach the twenty-first century, it has become evident that some fads and trends continue despite the passage of time. Individuals, who despite knowing the potential negative consequences associated with the use of illicit substances, continue to use various street drugs on a recreational basis. Psychoactive drugs have, indeed, increasingly become very much part of the mainstream of American life.[1] Social norms have been steadily changing to the point at which drugs are not only available, but in demand with a large supply. Obviously, we still live in a world that very much consists of thrill-seeking and risk-taking individuals who are willingly ready to experiment with a variety of illegal mind-altering compounds.

There have been ongoing investigations performed to determine why people use and/or resort to drugs. Some individuals choose to experiment with drugs to satisfy their curiosity of the unknown. Social pressures from peer, family, and societal role models still remain at the top of the list of reasons why adolescents take drugs.[2] Predisposition toward rebelliousness, nonconformity, and independence also figure prominently. A high correlation has also been found between parental drug use and abuse and drug abuse patterns among their children.[3] Some experimentation with mind-altering substances appears to be a part of the adolescent "rite of initiation" or "rite of passage."[4] There are also those who use drugs as a pathway for gaining insight, having fun, and creating a sense of belonging.[5]

Young people are for the most part curious and adventurous, and for some, drugs provide an opportunity to satisfy both.[6] To others, drug use offers an avenue of escape from specific pressures, everyday stress, and reality. Some individuals simply seek pleasure or heightened euphoria in their lives. Whatever the reason may be for drug use, individuals of all ages and backgrounds continue to ingest illicit substances regularly. It is believed that drug experimentation begins in the early adolescent years. One report pointed out that nearly two-thirds of all Americans have tried an illicit drug prior to finishing high school.[7] Various survey studies have shown that illicit drug use is on the decline; however, studies have suggested that Ecstasy use continues to reach epidemic proportions worldwide.[8-13]

In most instances, drug use begins in the pre-teen and teenage years, when individuals first experiment with the "gateway substances" (i.e., alcohol and cigarettes).[14] Since these gateway substances are more readily available than drugs sold on the illicit market, it is perfectly logical that these are the first to be taken. Illegal compounds are, however, becoming more readily available for individuals to buy, sell, and use—even to those who are still in their preteen years.

Although continued vigilant efforts are made to restrain people from using various substances, millions of individuals throughout the world consume illegal drugs regularly. While some believe individuals are not getting the message, others feel that the message is indeed being received, just ignored.[15] It is noteworthy that a majority of today's teenagers have at least experimented with an illegal drug some time during their lives. Even though a vast majority remain unscathed by their drug experiences,[9] various reports indicate that there are some who become both psychologically and physically incapacitated.

There has been relatively little public information with regard to the present substance of interest, Ecstasy. There has not been a formal movement toward specifically preventing Ecstasy use; however, it is believed that hundreds of thousands, perhaps millions, of individuals use this substance worldwide. The only information available to the public with regard to Ecstasy has come via newspaper reports, talk shows, and sporadic magazine feature stories. Outside of these mediums of communication, relatively little information about Ecstasy has been conveyed to the public.

A determined attempt is made in this work to provide readers with the facts surrounding Ecstasy. This book has been designed for readers worldwide who are curious about, tempted by, and uninformed or misinformed about the nature of Ecstasy and the consequences of its use.

INTRODUCING ECSTASY

The surge of LSD use throughout the better part of the 1960s led into several decades of more recent "drugs of choice," including 3,4-methylenedioxymethamphetamine (MDMA), or Ecstasy. This drug has had a long, yet traceable history. Most people do not know much about the birthplace of MDMA and its true origins. This chapter shall answer most, if not all, of the questions regarding the history of what we today refer to as Ecstasy.

Although MDM and M&M are sometimes used within the literature, MDMA is actually the most commonly used acronym for the chemical structure that bears the structural configuration of 3,4-methylenedioxymethamphetamine. Many people have never heard of MDMA; however, if the term "Ecstasy" or the letter "X" were to be mentioned, many are apt to nod and say that they have indeed heard of it or, in some instances, admit they have tried it. Although Ecstasy is the most commonly used nickname for MDMA, there have been various other street names used in place of MDMA, some of which sound as enticing as the names of perfumes shelved in department stores. The list of names includes XTC, Adam, M&M's, Mickey, Doctor, Love Doves, Rhapsody, Biscuits, and Raven; however, Ecstasy does remain the most common nickname for this substance. The letters "X" and "E" have also been commonly used to denote Ecstasy.

Ecstasy is a term that was actually coined well over a decade ago to describe the overall MDMA experience. The term "Empathy" had been originally proposed as a nickname for MDMA; however, Ecstasy was overwhelmingly most appealing to both the drug-using population and those who had been marketing the substance through clandestine—or concealed—manufacture.[16] Although it is virtually impossible to prove that MDMA is so popular because of its nickname, it is very conceivable that Ecstasy has been alluring to many of its users because of its name. Although the term Ecstasy remains consistently used on the streets among the general community, the term has been often used within the medical literature as well. Thus, MDMA and Ecstasy shall be used interchangeably throughout the context of this book.

HISTORICAL SIGNIFICANCE

Although popularly believed to have been synthesized as an appetite suppressant, MDMA was actually patented in Germany in the early 1900s as a precursor agent—or intermediate structural compound—possessing properties deemed to contain primary constituents for therapeutically active compounds.[17] Thus, the synthesis of MDMA was not performed as a means for developing a dietary agent, nor was it ever used for such purposes, as has been inaccurately reported.

The conveyance of MDMA as an "appetite suppressant" continues to be falsely reported throughout the lay press and medical literature. Myths, such as this one, typically begin when one author documents deceiving information, whereby others consequently just cite this information within their works. Nevertheless, MDMA was never used or intended to be used to curb appetite. Although Ecstasy can exert anorectic—or appetite suppressing—effects in some users,[18] it must be reiterated that this substance was never synthesized to produce such an effect.

Unfortunately, the public has been misinformed about the historical aspects of this substance, as well as various other factual information surrounding Ecstasy. This book, however, clears up much of the confusion that surrounds this increasingly popular recreational substance.

FACTS SURROUNDING MDMA SYNTHESIS

In its original patent, it is clearly documented that MDMA and other substances were synthesized as a means of determining the efficacy that certain compounds may have for therapeutic utilization. When the application for patenting MDMA was formulated in 1912, the intention was to determine if MDMA possessed key constituents that may serve as precursors for manufacturing potentially useful psychotherapeutic catalysts.

Although the application for patenting MDMA does not read "Merry Christmas," the original petition for its synthesis was made on Christmas Eve. Shortly thereafter, in 1914, the patent was issued. E. Merck in Darmstadt, Germany, is the pharmaceutical company that is responsible for having officially patented the drug. Although small modifications were made in the following five years,[19] the drug was never marketed and basically remained fallow—or ignored—for the following forty years.

EARLY LABORATORY STUDIES

Little attention had been focused upon this substance until the 1950s. During the early part of 1950, MDMA was used in a series of animal experiments done with the support of the United States Army.[20] This was basically the first time that this substance was closely scrutinized. Numerous lethal dose (LD_{50}) experiments were done on several nonhuman subjects, including mice, rats, guinea pigs, dogs, and monkeys. The toxicity of MDMA and several other phenylethylamines were assessed during the course of this particular study. Phenylethylamines are any of a series of compounds containing the phenylethylamine skeleton and modified by chemical constituents at appropriate positions in the molecule.

These LD_{50} studies were performed to determine the approximate administered dosage of each substance needed to kill these particular species. The findings were declassified in 1969 and published shortly thereafter. MDMA had been identified by the Edgewood Arsenal as experimental agent 1475 (EA-1475). The findings of this study demonstrated that MDMA, EA-1475, was one of the most toxic substances of those being investigated. However, MDMA was found to be less toxic in these animals when compared to another compound, 3,4-methylenedioxyamphetamine (MDA), a substance to which MDMA has often been compared. MDMA and MDA share many of the same anatomical properties. Further discussion of the structural significance of MDMA and MDA, as well as their relation, shall be discussed at greater length in Chapter 2.

There has been much written within the present body of scientific literature regarding the effects that MDMA has on brain neurotransmitter systems. Most of these laboratory studies involving the administration of MDMA have examined if and to what degree the substance has an effect on the brain neurotransmitter serotonin,[21] a key brain chemical responsible for the regulation of mood, sleep, sexual functioning, appetite, and depression. Although controversy continues regarding these types of animal studies and the assumptions made about humans, similar studies continue to be done in a wide range of arenas with not only MDMA, but hundreds of other drugs as well. The structural significance and mechanism of action of MDMA is completely depicted in Chapter 2.

ECSTASY USE

Human consumption of Ecstasy is believed to have first taken place in the latter part of the 1960s on the West Coast of the United States.[22] In the early 1970s, a laboratory in Chicago received drug specimens from the local police department. After a series of assays, it was determined that the substance was MDMA.[23] This report suggested that the substance had resurfaced. Furthermore, this report also indicated that MDMA was not only a substance of interest within laboratory settings, but also a drug being freely taken in recreational arenas by individuals in search of a spiritual high. During the same time period, another report stated that a "new classification" of drugs called phenylethylamines, such as MDMA, was being ingested by drug users.[24]

In the mid-1970s, an assay was performed in which MDMA was identified, thus further suggesting that MDMA had emerged among drug-using populations.[25] In the latter part of 1970, MDMA was introduced into the realm of psychotherapy on the West Coast and subsequently adopted by therapists on the East Coast.[26] Although little written documentation is available from MDMA-assisted psychotherapeutic sessions, several anecdotal accounts have suggested that the use of MDMA as an adjunct within therapy helped develop a mutual bond between the therapist and the client.[16,27] Due to the lack of blind or double-blind methodology, there has been difficulty in assessing the therapeutic efficacy of this compound. Therefore, it has been virtually impossible to substantiate the possible facilitative role that MDMA may have in a therapeutic context.

Psychiatrists reported that one MDMA-assisted therapy session could accomplish the equivalent of perhaps more than six months of the conventional approach.[28] Another report recapitulated how MDMA can bring hidden emotions and thoughts to the surface, thus enhancing empathy and trust.[29] Some psychiatrists believed that MDMA could play a legitimate role in therapy, giving credence to the substance for dissolving the ego's fears and defense mechanisms.[30] The use of therapeutically-active substances such as MDMA in psychotherapy is thoroughly discussed in Chapter 4.

The utilization of MDMA throughout the 1980s was not limited to therapeutic intervention. The euphoric effects that the drug elicits became widespread information, as MDMA became the "in drug" for many weekend party attendees. This substance quickly became referred to by its now infamous nickname, "Ecstasy."

A feature article, titled "Everything Looks Wonderful When You're Young and on Drugs," described the effects of Ecstasy and its widespread distribution.[31] Subsequent articles were printed in popular magazines regarding the sudden surge of Ecstasy use. One article described its efficacy in helping a woman confront her cancer less fearfully.[32] This same publication recited firsthand accounts of the drug experience, including that the drug makes one more accepting, self-assured, friendly, and loving. Another magazine story revealed that Ecstasy facilitated self-acceptance, self-love, contentment, tranquillity, insight, and an ability to "unravel psychological knots."[33] Ecstasy is described as being "the hottest thing in the continuing search for happiness through chemistry."[33]

With the increasing media attention being focused on this substance, it was only a matter of time before law enforcement and government officials intervened. In July 1986, MDMA was officially banned by the Drug Enforcement Administration (DEA). The action taken by the DEA presumably stemmed from the overwhelming reports suggesting that Ecstasy had become rampant in the public domain. The DEA voiced an immediate concern regarding this popular, yet possibly dangerous, unregulated substance. Although this substance was not necessarily viewed as being dangerous or lethal, the DEA was primarily concerned that this substance was being freely distributed on the streets, predominantly through clandestine manufacture without any control whatsoever. A lengthy hearing took place to determine if and what degree of control this substance needed. After several long and complex court hearings involving numerous issues and controversies, a final ruling was made that placed MDMA within Schedule I, the most restrictive of all drug classifications. The motion to ban MDMA as well as the entire legal proceedings leading to the prohibition of Ecstasy are discussed at length in Chapter 3.

Ecstasy has been increasingly popular throughout the past decade. The substance is taken recreationally, mainly for its euphoric properties. Ecstasy has, indeed, been the "drug of choice" for many years now, as its use has been very much linked with rave parties.[34-36] Raves are all-night parties in which people gather together in a particular location, usually under the influence of a mind-altering compound, most often Ecstasy. The recreational use of Ecstasy, as well as its association with raves, is described in Chapter 5. The adverse reactions ascribed to MDMA, ranging from short-term effects to fatal consequences, are extensively explained in Chapter 6 and Chapter 7.

The written contributions pertaining to Ecstasy have been predominantly negative—with the main message being "beware of the agony of Ecstasy." The persevering media hysteria about many drugs, including Ecstasy, attempts to dissuade individuals from using drugs. There have been, however, some lay-press articles and talk-show guests who have painted a much brighter image of Ecstasy. Great debate continues regarding this substance.

The Love Drug is a well-balanced book, capturing the historical aspects of this substance, as well as its dark, sometimes fatal side—including potential risks and actual tragedies associated with the use of MDMA—"Ecstasy." The following chapters provide detailed accounts of the emergence of this substance and its consequent shift from therapeutic utilization to recreational use.

Chapter 2

Terminology, Structural Significance, and Pharmacological Implications

TERMINOLOGY

Although Ecstasy is the most popular nickname for the chemical structure 3,4-methylenedioxymethamphetamine (MDMA), numerous names have been used on the street and recreational market to refer to this compound. Some of these names include XTC, Adam, M&M's, Mickey, Doctor, Love Doves, Rhapsody, Biscuits, and Raven. Often, the letters "X" and "E" have been used in short for Ecstasy. The literature and professional arenas have used various chemical names for this particular compound. Besides MDMA, the literature has included such names as N-methyl-beta-(3,4-methylenedioxyphenyl)-isopropylamine, N-methyl-3,4-methylenedioxyamphetamine, and 2-methylamine-1- (3,4-methylenedioxyphenyl)- propane.[1] In previous issues of *Chemical Abstracts,* this compound has been listed or documented as N, alpha-dimethyl-homopiperonylamine and N, alpha-dimethyl-3,4-methylenedioxyphenethylamine. The most recent *Chemical Abstracts* has indexed this compound as N, alpha-dimethyl-1,3-benzodioxole-5-ethanamine. Although this substance has had various nicknames and chemical references, it is noteworthy that there is only one chemical configuration represented.

Ecstasy has been incorrectly believed by some individuals to be a combination or admixture of several illicit substances including cocaine and heroin. Although the subjective effects of MDMA have been likened to mescaline and d-amphetamine, the idea that Ecstasy is a chemical blending of substances is completely false. In actuality, Ecstasy is a "pure" substance with its own chemical makeup.[2] The actual date on which MDMA was discovered and the manufacturing chemist remain unknown. Interestingly, MDMA and MDA were both originally synthesized at or about the same time in the early 1900s and remain listed on the same patent.[3]

Many papers in scientific literature have ambiguously classified the chemical structure of MDMA as a "designer drug." The common definition for a designer drug, however, does not describe the nature in which MDMA was first synthesized. Designer drugs have been defined as being "variations of already controlled synthetic drugs which mimic the effects of the classical narcotics, stimulants, and hallucinogens."[4] By this definition, designer drugs involve the process of reassembling an illicit compound, in essence creating an altered version so as to take on legal stature. Designer drugs have also been referred to as compounds that have been mainly synthesized for the purpose of circumventing—or avoiding—the laws.[5] According to these definitions of designer drugs, it would be inapt to label MDMA in this way.

Presumably, MDMA was believed to have been a restructured synthesis of 3,4-methylenedioxyamphetamine (MDA), a structurally similar compound to which MDMA has been often compared. MDA was banned in the early part of 1970, just a short time prior to the strong surge of Ecstasy use on the streets. It is very possible that recreational drug users resorted to MDMA following the prohibition of MDA; however, MDMA was never first manufactured or originally synthesized because of the banning of MDA. Since Ecstasy continues to be illegally manufactured by amateur chemists in private basements and bathtubs, the drug may be considered to be a clandestine substance, but still it is not a designer drug.

The mistaken classification of Ecstasy as a designer drug has presented this drug with a stigma, one which the drug has still not shaken. The false assumptions that have been publicly made about this compound may have indirectly or covertly contributed to the emergency scheduling of MDMA in the mid 1980s, as well as its subsequent permanent prohibition shortly thereafter (see Chapter 3). The Drug Enforcement Administration (DEA) has always been on the lookout for designer drugs, since various clandestine manufacturers attempt to alter compounds to "tip-toe" around the prohibition of certain substances. Even if MDMA was not falsely considered a designer drug, it may have eventually been placed in Schedule I anyway.

Although the media is concerned with educating, informing, and even influencing public opinion, widespread media reports have also been largely responsible for providing misleading notions about Ecstasy to society at large. Besides inaccurately referring to Ecstasy as a designer drug, the media have created further public confusion by associating Ecstasy with both overdoses and Parkinson's Disease,[6] when in fact there have been no cases of this nature reported to date. Specific works have been written with regard to the extensive and distorted information that the media have recited regarding Ecstasy. The misleading reports regarding the original intentions of MDMA, as well as some unfounded effects, have subsequently leaked out and appeared nationwide in the lay press and on worldwide televised news reports, stirring up widespread confusion and uncertainty about this substance.[7]

STRUCTURAL SIGNIFICANCE

MDMA is structurally similar to its parent compound, MDA. MDMA is actually the N-methyl derivative of MDA. Therefore, the structural change required in synthesizing MDMA is the addition of the one-carbon methyl group to the nitrogen. Although MDMA is a derivative of MDA and the two compounds share many of the same principal sources for their manufacture, this additional transformation (the added N-methyl group) makes these two substances markedly different.

Figure 2.1 and Figure 2.2 display the structural configurations of MDMA and MDA. This chemical transformation may seem insignificant when observing the structural makeup of these two substances; however, the differences between these substances are believed to become more salient when carefully comparing the respective pharmacological effects and implications. To equate MDMA with MDA based upon chemical similarity is rather misleading.

Although the added N-methyl group may, at first glance, appear minor or somewhat insignificant, this modification actually decreases the course of action of this substance when compared to hallucinogenic agents. The psychedelic or hallucinogenic properties have been reported as being removed from the active isomer upon the addition of this one-carbon methyl group.[8] In those particular instances when psychedelic compounds have been N-methylated, the hallucinogenic activity has been shown to be totally diminished or greatly reduced.[9]

FIGURE 2.1. Structure of MDMA

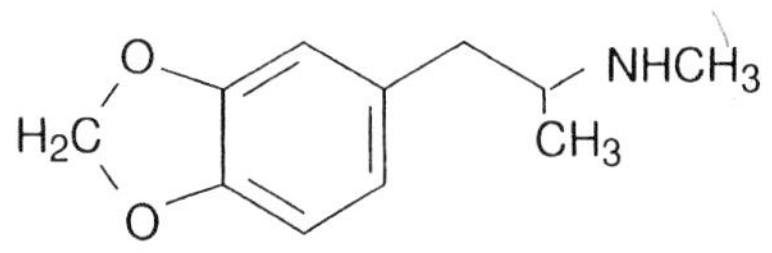

3,4-methylenedioxymethamphetamine (MDMA, Ecstasy)

FIGURE 2.2. Structure of MDA

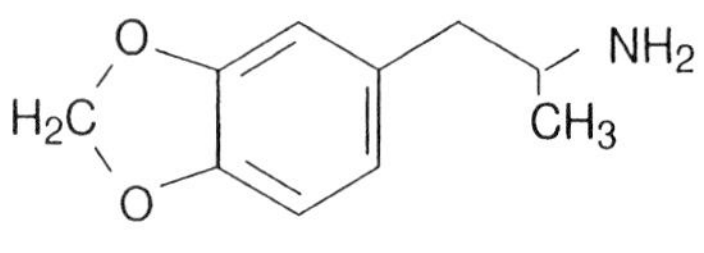

3,4-methylenedioxyamphetamine (MDA)

MDMA has been described as eliciting unique effects in its users; no other compound has been characterized in a manner similar to Ecstasy. The earliest published work to summarize the qualitative aspects of MDMA described the compound as producing an "altered state of consciousness with emotional and sensual overtones."[10] More recently, there has been a much broader cluster of passionate effects ascribed to Ecstasy (see Chapter 7). There are also several structural features that make MDMA quite unique. MDMA is 3,4-disubstituted. Both MDMA and MDA possess the 3,4-methylenedioxy function, where in fact there are no other compounds within the substituted amphetamine group that have substitution patterns only in the 3 and 4 positions. Another distinguishing feature of MDMA is that it is a secondary amine, with the basic nitrogen being substituted with an N-methyl. This configuration makes MDMA different from the hallucinogenic and amphetamine agents that are known for being most potent as primary amines.[11]

Besides the distinct structural features of MDMA, the effects that individuals have reported following use also sets this drug apart from others. The psychoactive effects of MDMA are quite different from classic psychostimulants and hallucinogenic agents. Although MDMA has been popularly classified as an "hallucinogenic-amphetamine," Ecstasy is not a potent stimulant, and hallucinations have rarely been reported to follow ingestion. Because of the particular nature of the effects that MDMA elicits, some have gone so far as to suggest that this substance may be worthy of being designated within its very own classification.[12] Many users have consistently reported specific subjective effects of MDMA including, but not limited to, its ability to facilitate communication, insight, love, conviviality, and euphoria.

Various studies have shown MDMA to be different from MDA in various respects. In animal studies, the LD_{50} determinations, the central analgesic effects, and the stimulatory actions were all quite different when comparing MDMA to MDA.[13] MDMA and MDA have been analyzed in the form of their respective optical isomers, R($-$)MDMA and S($+$)MDMA; R($-$)MDA and S($+$)MDA. The ($+$) and ($-$) are used to designate which direction the optical isomer, or enantiomer, will revolve on a plane of polarized light.[14] These analyses have also determined that the R($-$)-levorotatory-isomer is more active in MDA, while it is the S($+$)-dextrorotatory-isomer that is the more active in MDMA.[15] The active human dosage of MDMA and MDA also differ.

Findings have demonstrated that MDMA is less potent than MDA. Also, MDMA has been found to be less potent as a CNS agent when in its R-form, a finding which distinguishes this substance from hallucinogens, in which it is the R-enantiomer that is the more potent. Therefore, MDMA is not a close member of the structurally related hallucinogens. Furthermore, being that it is the S-isomer of MDMA that is more potent, this substance more closely resembles the activity of a stimulant. Lower doses of MDA may be comparable to the subjective effects of MDMA; at high doses, however, MDA may cause hallucinations, a neuropsychiatric phenomenon not associated with the use of MDMA. From the sparse published data, it could be interpreted that there may be some interaction between the two isomers of MDMA, in that the best presentation of activity seems to be with the racemate—the mixture of both enantiomers, ($+$)MDMA and ($-$)MDMA.[16] Table 2.1 depicts the pharmacological differences between these structurally related compounds.

Even though Ecstasy has not been known to evoke either auditory or visual hallucinations, it has often been classified as an "hallucinogenic-amphetamine." Classifying MDMA as an hallucinogenic compound within the same class as MDA, LSD, or PCP is an inappropriate designation, or in other words, a misnomer. As previously stated, Ecstasy is not known to cause hallucinations. There have been reports of hallucinations in a few

TABLE 2.1. MDMA and MDA Comparisons

	Psychedelic Action (R-form)	Racemic Mixture (50:50)	Stimulant Action (S-form)
MDA	R-MDA (120 mg) sensory harshness and long lived.	RS-MDA (120 mg) 60 mg of each form. The R-form is pre-dominant.	S-MDA (160 mg) more benign and peaceful.
MDMA	R-MDMA (200 mg), nearly inactive. 100 mg without any effects.	RS-MDMA (120 mg) 60 mg of each. The S-form is pre-dominant.	S-MDMA (120 mg) benign, with clear adrenergic effects.

Alexander T. Shulgin, 1985, unpublished table, adopted with permission.

instances in which individuals had used Ecstasy concomitantly with other drugs, or had consumed Ecstasy alone but in rather large quantities.[17]

Hallucinations, visual or auditory, have only rarely been associated with MDMA consumption. If and when hallucinations occur, many contributing factors must be considered, including: (1) the individual's mental health history; (2) possible concomitant use of other substances; and (3) the purity of MDMA ingested. To further elucidate the pharmacological effects of MDMA, more clinical studies are necessary.

Because MDMA has several features that distinguish it from both amphetamines and the classic hallucinogens, newer terms have been suggested as more appropriate categories for MDMA. "Empathogen," a term coined by Dr. Ralph Metzner, has been used to describe the effects that MDMA elicits.[18] Dr. Metzner believes that Empathogen is appropriate in describing MDMA, since its primary effects are emotional openness and empathy or sympathy. Few researchers or drug users have denied that MDMA possesses qualities that enhance empathy. On the other hand, Dr. David Nichols believes that the term Empathogen is somewhat inappropriate, mainly because MDMA, as well as other substances with similar pharmacological activity, does much more than produce empathy.[19] Dr. Nichols has referred to MDMA as an "Entactogen," a term that he believes better describes the drug. According to Dr. Nichols, Entactogen is a "neutral" term that has been observed as appropriate if the substance is to be used within a therapeutic context.[20] Furthermore, the therapist should be the one given credit for developing empathic communication during sessions, as opposed to relying on the drug ingestion alone.[21] Empathogen suggests that this drug, in and of itself, induces empathic communication. The term Entactogen has been used because of Ecstasy's ability to generate what has been described as "touching from within."

Nevertheless, both Empathogen and Entactogen have been commonly used as classifications for MDMA and other substances that help increase openness and empathy and enhance insight. Realistically, however one decides to classify Ecstasy is really a matter of choice. What remains apparent is that Ecstasy has a stimulating effect on the central nervous system in a majority of its users, while also inducing sensations that have been characterized as predominantly euphoric or blissful.

MECHANISMS OF DRUG ACTION AND NEUROTOXICITY

The recent surge in Ecstasy use has inspired a great deal of research into delineating the mechanisms of action of this substance. The central mechanism of drug action has yet to be fully substantiated. There have been, however, numerous works written within the preclinical literature regarding the putative mechanisms of MDMA. Although its exact drug actions are not fully known, pharmacological studies have demonstrated that MDMA produces a central stimulant-like effect that appears to be mediated by brain monoamines, including serotonin and dopamine.

Although there is a complexity of neurotransmitter involvement during the action of MDMA, the pharmacological effects of

MDMA are believed to be primarily mediated via serotonergic mechanisms.[22] MDMA is a serotonergic agonist, well known for its ability to release serotonin in a potent manner and subsequently block serotonin reuptake in various brain regions.[23,24] MDMA has demonstrated to be particularly potent at various serotonin recognition sites, allegedly altering serotonergic transmission at both post- and presynaptic serotonin receptors.[25] MDMA has been shown to block the reuptake of dopamine as well, though to a lesser extent.[26,27]

Other potent serotonin-releasing agents have not elicited the rewarding psychoactive effects typically associated with Ecstasy. This would suggest that there are other mediating neurotransmitter implications besides MDMA-induced serotonin release.[28] Although brain serotonin may indeed have a primary role in mediating the effects of Ecstasy, other neurotransmitter networks (e.g., dopamine and norepinephrine) may also contribute, alone or with serotonin, to elicit the euphoria, social closeness, increased sensuality, and other unique subjective phenomena following Ecstasy consumption.

Serotonergic stimulation typically occurs shortly following administration of the drug ($\leq$30 minutes), with dopaminergic stimulation happening sometime thereafter.[29,30] MDMA has been reported to act in a biphasic manner on serotonergic neurotransmitter systems.[31,32] During the first stage, the initial effects produce marked increases of serotonin release. Following these vigorous discharges of serotonin, ongoing synthesis has been shown to be inhibited. Significant reductions in brain serotonin concentrations have been found shortly following MDMA administration (three to six hours). These initiatory effects appear to produce changes in serotonin that are for the most part purported to be reversible. In the second stage (twenty-four hours to one week), the prolonged effects of MDMA become profound, with significant damage to serotonin nerve terminals characterized by substantial loss of serotonin reuptake sites.

These subsequent degenerative effects on serotonergic neurons have been irreversible in many instances.

Studies have demonstrated that MDMA significantly alters neurotransmitter functioning and causes drastic neurodegenerative effects on serotonergic function. Monoamine levels have been shown to be altered in a region-specific and dose-dependent manner following MDMA treatment.[33,34] MDMA also causes neurodegeneration of serotonergic uptake sites, as well as marked reductions in the activity of tryptophan hydroxylase, the rate-limiting enzyme of serotonin synthesis.[35,36]

Serotonergic neurotoxicity following MDMA treatment has been demonstrated in a variety of experimental animals. Studies have revealed that MDMA is neurotoxic to serotonergic nerve fibers in rats, mice, guinea pigs, and monkeys.[37,38] One MDMA-related study utilizing dogs revealed that this substance may not only be neurotoxic, but also deadly, as one dog died shortly following one administered dose (15 mg/kg) of MDMA.[39] MDMA causes predictable dose-related reductions of brain serotonin and 5-hydroxyindoleacetic acid (5-HIAA), the primary serotonin metabolite.[36,40] Significant decreases in concentrations of 5-HIAA have been consistently found in laboratory animals following MDMA administration.[41] One study found concentrations of 5-HIAA in human cerebrospinal fluid to be significantly reduced in individuals who have had prior exposure to MDMA.[42] A different study, however, did not find MDMA users to have decreased levels of 5-HIAA.[43]

Although there have been relatively few investigations performed to analyze adrenergic implications, MDMA has also been described as being an adrenergic agonist as well.[51] Clinically, this compound has displayed remarkable sympathomimetic activity including, yet not limited to, peripheral vasoconstrictions, tachycardia, pupil dilation, and effects on other smooth muscles.[44] The mechanism of neuronal toxicity remains unclear but may be at least partially due to the stimulation of peripheral and central adrenergic receptor activity.[45] It is believed that MDMA is especially potent at adrenergic receptors.[46]

Selective serotonin reuptake inhibitor (SSRI) agents, including fluoxetine (Prozac), have been efficaciously used in treating Ecstasy-induced side effects in humans.[47] SSRI medications have been known to selectively inhibit CNS neuronal uptake of serotonin, thus allowing for homeostatic serotonin neurotransmission. It is not suggested that Ecstasy users simultaneously ingest SSRI agents or other medications as prophylactic measures to the potential side effects of Ecstasy.[48] MDMA has various neurotransmitter implications besides serotonin; thus, these supposed prophylactic agents may do little in counteracting the wide range of potential personal and biological complications.

CONCLUDING NOTES

MDMA is a unique substance with distinct structural and pharmacological characteristics. MDMA, or Ecstasy, has been referred to by various nicknames and chemical terminology. This substance has only one structural configuration, however, and is not a concoction of illicit substances.

Prior to 1985, this substance had been professionally manufactured in the laboratories of renowned chemists. Since being banned, however, MDMA has mostly been synthesized within clandestine laboratories—among the "underground" drug market. The principal sources used in the synthesis of MDMA are piperonal, isosafrol, safrole, and piperonylacetone.[1] Both professional chemists and underground unlicensed manufacturers have used the same scientific procedures to yield this compound. Although clandestine manufacturers have followed the very same preparations as those used when the drug was legal,[49-51] the underground market still does warrant concern for prospective users. Whenever drugs are manufactured on the clandestine market, there are always concerns regarding quality and purity.

Controversy surrounds MDMA-related animal studies, since considerably higher doses are administered in experimental investigations compared to the dosages typically consumed by humans.[52] The notion of extrapolating animal research findings to humans has long been debated. Presently, there is insufficient data to determine if, and to what extent, MDMA is neurotoxic in humans. The possible irreversible or prolonged degenerative effects that MDMA has on serotonin function is of particular concern because there is widespread human consumption of this substance.

Although environmental considerations (i.e., set and setting) are believed to influence the effects of MDMA, Ecstasy alone appears to affect central monoamine levels independent of confounding factors. Furthermore, MDMA is believed to exert central stimulant-like effects and possible serotonergic neurotoxicity regardless of environmental determinants. Various adverse symptomatologies, presumed to be serotonin-related, have been reported to follow MDMA use.[53] It must be emphasized that MDMA-induced alterations to serotonin mechanisms may not be limited to only laboratory animals.

Chapter 3

MDMA/Ecstasy
and Legal Implications

It has been a decade since Ecstasy was placed into the most restrictive drug categorization, Schedule I. There does, however, continue to be a great deal of controversy and confusion surrounding the prohibition of this substance. MDMA continues to be of great interest to various professionals, researchers, and general community members alike. This chapter describes the sequence of events that occurred along the pathway toward the permanent banning of what was once considered to be a medical breakthrough.

ECSTASY ON THE LICIT MARKET

Throughout the 1970s, MDMA-assisted psychotherapy was being advocated by psychotherapists who believed that the substance facilitated the healing process.[1] The substance was administered within the scope of psychotherapy under the direction and guidance of attending psychotherapists. MDMA was lobbied by mental health professionals who believed in the ability of this substance to provide sensory and spiritual benefits to those who sought help. The substance was utilized for several years by practitioners nationwide with few, if any, subjective or objective contraindications reported.

In the early 1980s, Ecstasy emerged upon the recreational scene, not only used by weekend party goers, but also freely sold in partylike atmospheres. Reports out of Dallas, Texas, suggested that Ecstasy, the so-called "Love Drug," was purchased with cash and even credit cards by patrons entering clubs and bars.[2] Club owners and individuals tending the bar were reported to have warmly received these customers, as Ecstasy was a popular and easy sale and, moreover, still legal. A bar in Houston, Texas, supposedly was distributing Ecstasy free of charge.[3] Anecdotal reports have also revealed that Ecstasy was readily available for those interested in experimenting with this mind-altering substance.

MOTION TO BAN ECSTASY

In 1984, Lloyd Bentsen, U.S. Senator from Texas, made a formal request to the DEA to ban the drug Ecstasy. The first notice indicated the proposed action was to not only make the drug illegal, but to place the substance into the strictest of all drug classifications, Schedule I.

This announcement specifically stated that:

> In the event that comments, objections, or requests for hearing raise one or more issues which the Administrator finds warrant a hearing, the Administrator shall order a public hearing by notice in the Federal Register.[4]

This touched off a two-year debate of oral and written testimony regarding the legislation of MDMA. The rigorous involvement of several individuals on behalf of both camps soon became quite apparent.

In response to this first notice, and much to the surprise of the DEA, several interested professors, physicians, and psychologists came forward in strong opposition to this proposed Schedule I placement of MDMA. Shortly thereafter, a follow-up notice was listed revealing that sixteen responses were received in answer to the proposed scheduling, with seven requesting formal hearings.[5] These individuals, who shall be called advocates, were very much opposed to a Schedule I classification for MDMA, which in turn would ultimately halt MDMA-assisted therapy and disrupt continued research endeavors. These advocates were driven by the belief that MDMA could be used within the realm of therapy when monitored, a sentiment contradictory to the DEA's position that MDMA had no currently accepted medical utility, regardless of the presence of professional supervision.

On November 14, 1984, the Administrator of the DEA, John Lawn, delegated the matter and court proceedings to the Administrative Law Judge, Francis L. Young. Judge Young was to conduct the hearings and gather all of the factual evidence presented on this case. Judge Young was instructed to report to John Lawn as to what he felt would be the most appropriate scheduling action with respect to MDMA upon the completion of ongoing investigations and both written and oral submissions.

Howard McClain, Chief of the DEA, explained the procedures involved in Administrative Law Hearings in the following way:

> The Administrative Law Judge presides over the hearings and gathers the complete record from both parties. After the hearings conclude, the judge is required to make a recommendation to the acting Administrator, in this case John C. Lawn. Upon hearing the recommendation made by the judge, it is the sole discretion of the Administrator to either accept or refuse the proposal made. Although the Administrative Law Judge presides over the hearing, the Administrator may intervene at his or her discretion in unusual circumstances.[6]

On February 1, 1985, a preliminary hearing took place regarding the proceedings on the proposed scheduling of MDMA. This preliminary meeting consisted of discussions pertaining to the instructions required of each witness and the issues to be discussed throughout the hearings in their entirety.[7] The attending attorneys in this case were Stephen Stone, attorney representing the DEA, and Richard Cotton, attorney speaking on behalf of the active MDMA advocates. The hearings subsequently were scheduled and assigned to take place in California, Missouri, and Washington, DC.

When the Administrator of the DEA ordered that MDMA be placed in Schedule I of the Controlled Substance Act (CSA) on a temporary basis, he had believed that such action was necessary to avoid an imminent hazard to the safety of the community during the course of the hearings.[8] Not only was there ongoing concern that this substance may have a potential for abuse, but also fear that MDMA may cause short-term or perhaps permanent brain changes as well. The Administrator stated that MDMA would be placed temporarily in Schedule I, effective July 1, 1985, and remain within this Schedule classification until a more concrete ruling was made. The ruling would be based on lengthy courtroom proceedings with testimonies of witnesses from both parties.

On one side of the controversy surrounding the scheduling of MDMA were many advocates who reiterated the beneficial uses of MDMA within monitored settings. Psychiatrists and other medical professionals were also quick to become involved in the Administrative Law Hearings on behalf of this substance. This pro-MDMA faction believed that the drug had therapeutic value, with no legitimate concerns for abuse if taken in a proper context (i.e., supervised therapeutic settings). Because MDMA was deemed to have been successfully administered in medical practices, several psychiatrists and other mental health workers strongly objected to the strict and sudden scheduling of MDMA.

On the other side were witnesses who testified on behalf of the DEA. These individuals assertively voiced their perspectives regarding MDMA's abuse potential and its lack of medical safety. This opposing faction consisted of individuals who believed that MDMA should be scheduled, primarily due to its purported "high" potential for abuse. This faction included individuals very much in favor of the banning of MDMA. This opposing group of individuals mainly formed their beliefs based upon laboratory findings that demonstrated that a similar substance, methylenedioxyamphetamine (MDA), causes sufficient reductions in the levels of brain serotonin in nonhumans.[9] As mentioned in earlier chapters, MDA has often been considered synonymous with MDMA; therefore, the experimental findings of MDA were brought into evidence as the DEA attempted to put MDMA under even greater scrutiny. Although animal studies attempt to predict the effects that drugs have in humans, experimental evidence and the entire notion of extrapolating animal research findings to humans continues to remain controversial.

Numerous court hearings took place during 1984 and 1986, until MDMA was permanently outlawed by the DEA. A final ruling was made that resulted in the everlasting placement of MDMA into Schedule I of CSA, effective November 13, 1986. The following paragraphs contain a detailed review of specific testimonial evidence offered by these opposing factions.

THE MDMA ADVOCATES

Various testimony was presented on behalf of MDMA and its utility in medical practice. MDMA was distinguished from MDA, the compound found to produce withstanding damage in the brains of nonhuman subjects. Dr. Lester Grinspoon noted that MDMA elicits less change in consciousness and is a much milder drug than MDA, with an even shorter duration. MDMA was also presented as having the capacity to help people get in touch with inner feelings and to facilitate the recalling of early memories.[10] Professor Thomas Roberts testified that MDMA may be used as immediate intervention during depression, comparing it to other antidepressants which take days, sometimes weeks, to be effective.[11]

The largest portion of testimony pertaining to MDMA-assisted therapy was provided by Dr. George Greer, a psychiatrist who had allegedly used MDMA with success within his medical practice. The affidavit given by this individual explained how MDMA had been efficacious for numerous individuals who had taken the substance in controlled settings. An unpublished manuscript was presented depicting the numerous benefits reported by twenty-nine subjects who had taken part in an investigative study.[12] The subjects had also reported a variety of sympathomimetic effects upon ingesting MDMA; however, all of the participants reported advantageous outcomes from their MDMA experiences.

Dr. Greer believed in the therapeutic potential of MDMA, although the substance had not been "scientifically proven" through double-blind studies.[13] Dr. Greer expressed his position on this matter in the following way:

> I would like to draw a distinction here between a scientifically proven effective treatment and a medically acceptable treatment. Many treatments, especially in psychiatry, are accepted by many practitioners, but have not been proven to be effective to the satisfaction of all scientists in the field. The efficacy of psychotherapy itself, with its myriad techniques, has yet to be scientifically proven to be effective to the satisfaction of many psychiatrists and psychologists. Yet, it is considered to be medically accepted treatment. It is my clinical judgment, and that of my peer review committee, that based on my clinical experience, the use of MDMA is a medically accepted part of the treatment approach I use.

Dr. Greer, a psychiatrist, and Requa Tolbert, a psychiatric nurse, had used MDMA with their patients on numerous occasions during the course of psychotherapy. Many of their reports suggested that MDMA helped facilitate communication, while decreasing clients' inhibitions. This substance supposedly enabled people to discuss various issues freely and helped people have a clear understanding of their presenting problems. Furthermore, MDMA was reported to have been useful for helping patients receive constructive criticism and accept the simplest of compliments.[14] A personal letter to Dr. Greer was also used as evidence in providing in-depth detail regarding the salient differences that exist when comparing MDMA to MDA.[15]

Further testimony included that of Dr. Robert Lynch, a psychiatrist, who described MDMA as one of the best "mind-exploring" substances available.[16] This witness also testified that MDMA ingestion does not cause any loss of reality. Another MDMA advocate, Dr. Phillip Wolfson, declared a genuine concern for the continued livelihood of MDMA, reporting that MDMA had been used successfully in cases of severe emotional distress. Wolfson also stated that MDMA had a low potential for abuse and had appeared to be efficacious for treating a wide range of psychiatric disorders, including psychosis.[17]

Dr. Rick Strassman, assistant professor of psychiatry at the University of New Mexico, suggested that MDMA is not a true psychedelic compound. He also noted that although animal studies may demonstrate toxicity following immense administrations of MDMA, the scientific evidence did not support that MDMA had ever been or would be highly abused or likely to induce toxic effects in humans. Dr. Strassman also claimed that there had been no data supporting the notion that MDMA may evoke "untoward and unsafe physical and psychological reactions."[18] Moreover, Dr. Strassman pointed out that even with the acceptance of the rather large speculative figures of MDMA dosage distribution, the reports of adverse reactions to MDMA remain rare. Dr. Strassman explained how the lack of double-blind methodology did not mean that MDMA lacked medical utility.

Many have continued to be dissatisfied with the illegal status of MDMA and the reasoning behind its criminalization. Dr. Alexander Shulgin, renowned researcher, recounts a number of "questionable maneuvers" that were made during the 1980s, as the emergency scheduling of MDMA was considered to have been most essential.[19] Dr. Shulgin, and fellow proponents of MDMA, believed that the substance should indeed be a controlled substance; however, at the same time, they found Schedule I to be an inappropriate categorization for this particular substance, considering its supposed advantageous use during therapy. These individuals believed Schedule III of the CSA to be a more appropriate placement, in that such placement would have enabled MDMA to be readily used for both medical treatment and scientific research, while still curtailing recreational consumption.

Schedule I is the most confining drug category of the CSA. In order for a drug to be placed within Schedule I, the CSA requires that a drug (1) have a high potential for abuse, (2) have no practical utility for treatment, and (3) have no accepted safety for medical utilization even when in the presence of professional supervision. These three criteria must be met prior to the placing of a drug within a Schedule I confinement. Table 3.1 contains the entire list of CSA classifications and category criteria for the different schedules (Schedule I-Schedule V).

Contrary to the criteria necessary for a Schedule I categorization, many believed that there had been no supporting evidence to suggest any dangers associated with Ecstasy consumption prior to the court hearings. Paradoxically, several reports had suggested that MDMA had been used successfully as an adjunct during therapy and the overall healing process, with no reports of deleterious or fatal reactions.

THE OPPOSING ARGUMENTS

There were several individuals who came forward in rebuttal to the testimony offered by the advocates of MDMA. Responses in opposition to legalizing MDMA were given in written form, as well as through direct court appearances. Dr. Harlan Shannon testified that although double-blind placebo studies could have been performed, no such studies had been attempted.[20] Dr. Shannon also suggested that since there were no "valid" clinical reports of MDMA, there existed a need to rely on the available animal data, which were unfavorable.

TABLE 3.1. Controlled Substance Act (CSA) Classifications

Schedule	Criteria
Schedule I	a. High potential for abuse
	b. No currently acceptable medical use in treatment
	c. Lack of accepted safety for use under medical supervision
Schedule II	a. High potential for abuse
	b. Currently accepted medical use
	c. Abuse may lead to severe physical or psychological dependence
Schedule III	a. Potential for abuse less than I and II
	b. Currently accepted medical use
	c. Abuse may lead to moderate physical dependence or high psychological dependence
Schedule IV	a. Low potential for abuse relative to III
	b. Currently accepted medical use
	c. Abuse may lead to limited physical or psychological dependence relative to III
Schedule V	a. Low potential for abuse relative to IV
	b. Currently accepted medical use
	c. Abuse may lead to limited physical or psychological dependence relative to IV

Dr. Joel Kleinman, a psychiatrist with a strong background in research, also testified that the MDMA studies performed had lacked scientific merit. Dr. Kleinman believed that the findings were inundated with the researchers' expectations, thus lacking objectivity.[21]

Dr. Kleinman found that the previous MDMA studies had all lacked credibility and scientific merit. Five major points were brought to the foreground as to why these MDMA studies were ultimately meaningless. Dr. Kleinman listed his points in the following manner: (1) there were no adequate descriptions of the patients or subjects of the studies; (2) these investigations did not incorporate blind or double-blind methodology; (3) there were no objective outcome criteria for which measurement conclusions could be drawn in an unbiased manner; (4) the studies appear to be heavily biased; and (5) the reports are almost entirely anecdotal and, thus, largely subjective. In essence, the studies were viewed as being "scientifically unsound."

Dr. Lewis Seiden also testified on behalf of the government. Dr. Seiden's affidavit included comparisons of MDMA to several other compounds, particularly MDA.[22] Based on the effects that MDA had on rats following excessive administered doses, he hypothesized that MDMA would have similar, or perhaps, the same neurotoxic effects on other animal species and would pose potential hazards to humans as well. Dr. Seiden, during his direct testimony, explained that:

> 3,4-methylenedioxymethamphetamine (MDMA) may be toxic to serotonin (5-hydroxytryptamine, 5-HT) neurons in the human brain. If so, this would be serious because 5-HT cells are believed to play a major role in pain perception, sleep, and affect the regulation and expression of aggressive and sexual behavior.
>
> In a drug trial, the preliminary case for efficacy must be weighed against the potential for harmful side effects. The case to date that MDMA is an effective drug seems weak; furthermore, there is evidence to suggest that the drug could harm 5-HT cells in the brain.[22]

Dr. Seiden also explained that when studies are performed on drugs, they should be performed in a systematic and well-controlled manner, as is usually done under an Investigational New Drug Permit.

Dr. Ronald Siegel attested that the nonmedical use of MDMA in the United States had risen from an estimated 10,000 doses distributed in the year 1976 to 30,000 doses distributed per month in 1985, thus suggesting that MDMA was being frequently taken within recreational atmospheres. Dr. Siegel concluded that:

MDMA has no currently accepted proven medical use in treatment in the United States. Thus far, case reports and clinical observations, albeit suggestive, are insufficient for demonstrating treatment effectiveness.[23]

Dr. Siegel further declared:

MDMA can be unsafe in nonmedical patterns of use. Since many of the untoward physical and psychological reactions contributing to this lack of street safety are also reported to occur in medical settings, it is doubtful that present medical and pharmacological knowledge can always supervise use with acceptable safety.[23]

Dr. Siegel also reminded a public media source about a story of some unknown therapist in Chicago who was found directing traffic after having supposedly taken Ecstasy. Although this isolated traffic incident was anecdotal, there was no hesitation in bringing this to widespread media attention and incorporating it into important legal testimony.[24]

Other direct testimony brought into question pertained to whether MDMA could have even demonstrated any true efficacy given that the substance had been administered during uncontrolled investigations. Dr. John Docherty stated that in order for MDMA to be considered therapeutically useful, it would have been necessary for at least one group to have been receiving MDMA and a control group(s) not on the receiving end of the compound.[25] In other words, in order for such a study to have been viewed as scientifically performed, it would have been essential to have had a control group who had not received MDMA, but rather a placebo.

Dr. Docherty also pointed out that such studies must comply with the necessary and well-documented scientific standards, unlike these investigations in which the professional procedures were not properly followed. Dr. Docherty, in his testimony, characterized the previous studies as "inadequate," because the investigations had been very casually done without exercising the proper procedures necessary to determine the efficacy of a substance among humans. The methodology used was described as troublesome, since no reasonable foundation existed to conclude that MDMA is therapeutically effective.

Testimony on behalf of the DEA also stated that the procedures had not been followed even though several therapists had been freely administering MDMA to various individuals. Typically, an evaluation of a substance begins with an investigational new drug application, whereby a series of procedures are performed to determine if, and under what circumstances, a substance shall be legally administered to humans.[26] The investigational new drug application process, which has been in effect since 1938, requires that specific procedures be followed prior to the marketing of a new substance. It was explained that although this action demands that several criteria be adhered to before a drug is marketed, none of these standards were followed in an attempt to appropriately and professionally manufacture and market MDMA.

RECOMMENDATION AND FINAL RULING

On May 22, 1986, Judge Francis L. Young made the long-awaited recommendation regarding these MDMA hearings. After having reviewed the entire record, both oral and written testimony, Judge Young concluded that MDMA should be placed within Schedule III as opposed to Schedule I where the DEA camp had wanted MDMA to be placed. A Schedule III placement would allow for MDMA-assisted psychotherapy and continued research endeavors. Judge Young, in his closing summary, explained that MDMA, prior to being proscribed, did have what he believed to be a currently acceptable use in treatment. Judge Young also concluded that MDMA did have acceptable safety levels when used under medical supervision. Finally, this Administrative Law Judge stated that the evidence of record did not establish that MDMA had a "high potential for abuse."[27] In short, Judge Young found that MDMA had not met any of the three criteria necessary for a Schedule I placement and made an emphatic recommendation to the Administrator to place this compound within Schedule III. As mentioned earlier, a drug must fulfill each of the three criteria in order to be a Schedule I substance.

According to a Schedule I status, a substance must have a high potential for abuse. However, MDMA users report that with increasing use of this substance, undesirable effects become pre-dominant. Studies of Ecstasy consumption have revealed that most users tend to ingest only small quantities of this compound since repeat doses induce increased side effects, in contrast to extending the pleasurable high. MDMA has been openly classi-fied as "nonaddictive," which would, in fact, contradict the notion that MDMA has a high potential to be abused.[3] Moreover, studies have shown that the positive effects tend to diminish with increased usage.[28] It is uniformly believed that many written laws pertaining to drugs and drug scheduling are vague in their definitions of "abuse" and "medical utility." Nonetheless, Judge Young gathered the complete record, including his own findings and concluding recommendations, and handed the mat-ter over to the DEA Administrator for a final ruling.

With still more testimony to be heard, another notice was published which indicated that there was going to be an exten-sion of the temporary confinement of MDMA within Schedule I.[29] This extension was ordered to maintain MDMA within Schedule I for an additional six months or until the proceedings had been completed. The Administrator realized that more time would be necessary for the government to document their excep-tions to the findings made by the Administrative Law Judge.

There was some disagreement regarding the Administrative Law Judge's opinions and recommendations. A member of the controlled substances board immediately filed concerns with the

DEA Administrator.[30] This affidavit discussed concerns pertaining to the recommendation of Judge Young to place MDMA within Schedule III, despite lacking a new drug application. It pointed out how this Administrative Law Judge had failed to determine the meaning of "accepted medical use," claiming that Judge Young should have recognized that the acceptance of a drug must first be done by the FDA, at which time the decision to administer MDMA to humans would be made.

After a thorough overview of the entire hearings and the Administrative Law Judge's recommendation, the Administrator ruled that MDMA met all of the criteria necessary for placement into Schedule I. The Administrator reviewed the entire record on the matter and refused to accept the recommendation that had been made to him by his own Administrative Law Judge. Although Judge Young did not believe that MDMA fulfilled any of the criteria worthy of a Schedule I legislation, the Administrator found Schedule I to be the obvious placement for this compound.

In the latter part of 1986, the decision was affirmed that MDMA should remain a Schedule I substance.[31] As a result, MDMA was given permanent illicit status and confined within the most restrictive category of the CSA. A short time after, however, MDMA was temporarily removed from Schedule I so that the Administrator could reevaluate the scheduling procedures, effective December 22, 1987.[32] After further review, it was concluded that MDMA had been appropriately placed in Schedule I. Without delay, the substance was placed back in Schedule I, with the effective date being March 23, 1988.[33]

DISCUSSION

As a result of the original emergency scheduling and follow-up prohibition final ruling, doctors were no longer able to legally prescribe MDMA within their practice of medicine, and MDMA was no longer shelved in the offices of psychiatrists. The

proponents of this substance found that the unfortunate consequence of this course of action was not only that MDMA was no
longer available for medical intervention, but more important,
that MDMA became and still remains practically inaccessible for
research investigations on humans. From the standpoint of these
MDMA supporters, much of the controversy seems to have risen
from the act of "placing research and potential medical therapeutic prescription out of practical reach."[34] As MDMA continues
to reach epidemic proportions among drug-using populations
throughout the country, researchers must await special permission to study this substance.

Reports had surfaced well before the Administrative Law
Hearings suggesting that the substance possessed medical utility.
Sophia Adamson, in her book *Through the Gateway of the Heart,*
documented several cases in which MDMA had been beneficial
for therapeutic purposes.[35] These anecdotal cases were supposed
to have demonstrated the medical utility of MDMA; however, no
substance can be legally considered for medical use unless the
compound is subjected to carefully controlled studies performed
in a scientific and objective manner.

MDMA faced a great deal of scrutiny throughout the hearings
because this substance had never been scientifically and professionally examined through double-blind methodology with a control group used for the purposes of comparison. For a substance to
demonstrate medical effectiveness, it must be shown to have statis-
tically greater beneficial outcomes for those receiving the compound compared to those individuals in the control group who had
not been receiving the drug. The experimental findings, along with
the lack of double-blind studies, were evidently sufficient for the
Administrator to overlook and override the recommendation made
by his Administrative Law Judge, Francis L. Young.

The scheduling of MDMA is of great interest because after
two years of both verbal and written testimony, the recommendation made by the Administrative Law Judge that MDMA belongs

in Schedule III fell on deaf ears. On the other hand, there still remain many who believed and continue to believe that MDMA belongs within the confines of a Schedule I placement.

Criticisms are bound to arise with the scheduling of drugs. The drug legalization debate has been in effect for some time now. The opposing viewpoints for drugs in general, as well as MDMA in particular, are illustrated in the following tables (see Table 3.2 and Table 3.3).

TABLE 3.2. Arguments for and Against the Legalization of Illicit Drugs

Advocates	Opponents
People have always used and will continue to use illicit drugs.	Continued illicit drug use does not justify legalizing a harmful activity.
People have the right to pursue behavior that may be harmful to them as long as it does not affect others.	Use of illicit drugs does affect others in a harmful multitude of ways unrelated to their legal status.
Current enforcement has little impact on criminal activities and only a slight deterrent effect.	Enforcement has not been effective due to the manner in which it has been pursued.
Crime would decrease as the cost of drugs would plummet.	If drugs were more readily available, use would increase, productivity would decrease, and crime might well increase.
Legalization would not be accompanied by an inordinate increase in drug use.	The potential for increase in drug use is enormous.
Legalization would still not permit access to drugs by children.	At present, children's access to alcohol and tobacco is rampant. Access to other drugs would be similarly difficult to control.
If drugs were legalized, education would prevent individuals from knowingly using substances with adverse effects.	The mere act of legalizing drugs implies a certain approval by society. The complications of these drugs would be trivialized.

Source: Barry Stimmel. *Drug Abuse and Social Policy in America,* 1996, New York: The Haworth Press, Inc. Table 3.2 adapted with permission.

TABLE 3.3. Arguments for and Against Legalizing MDMA (Ecstasy)

Advocates	Opponents
People have used and will continue to use Ecstasy regardless of its legal status.	Continued use of MDMA does not justify legalizing this potentially dangerous drug.
The legalization of Ecstasy would allow for the pure and professional synthesis of MDMA, as opposed to adultered, perhaps lethal, compound replacements.	While the professional synthesis would decrease the chances of contaminated MDMA tablets, legalization would convey a misleading message that this drug is safe.
MDMA has potential for medical use and the capacity to be used successfully as an adjunct for psychotherapy.	MDMA lacks medical use and has the potential to be extremely abused.
The legalization of MDMA would enable more research endeavors on this substance.	Legalization would have no effect on research efforts.
MDMA has been shown to be efficacious for treating individuals who have family difficulties, trauma, terminal illness, addictions, phobias, and other disorders.	MDMA has not been proven to be medically useful through scientific evaluations using a control group, a placebo, and double-blind methodology.
MDMA has not been shown to cause long-term brain damage in humans. Also, the experimental findings in animals should not be extrapolated to humans, especially considering that the experimental dosages are excessively high.	MDMA has been shown to cause obvious brain alterations in experimental studies. The effects that MDMA and similar structured compounds have on serotonin regulated systems warrants concern.

CONCLUDING COMMENTS

It is widely believed that the Administrator placed a great deal of emphasis on testimony regarding animal studies, even though the CSA makes no mention of extrapolating such evidence in making legislative decisions. In this particular court proceeding pertaining to Ecstasy, two major extrapolations were made: (1) since MDMA and MDA are similar in structure, it was believed that MDMA may evoke similar brain alterations and anomalies; (2) the experiments were done using laboratory animals rather than humans. Therefore, when MDMA was found to cause brain-altering effects in animals, it was simply presumed that similar brain destruction would occur in humans as well. Furthermore, although MDMA and MDA are structurally quite similar, their pharmacological mechanisms have been found to be quite distinct. Second, not only were the MDMA experiments conducted in animals, but the doses administered to these animals greatly exceeded the body weight proportion of that typically consumed by humans. Thus, these extrapolations remain troublesome in various respects.

During the past decade, MDMA has been attributed to numerous organic complications. In the most extreme instances, such anomalies have resulted in death. The substance is indeed capable of adversely affecting bodily function, at least when its use is unmonitored. MDMA is not necessarily believed to be a safe drug; however, many believe that the placement of MDMA has been driven on pure speculation.

The decision to immediately ban MDMA has remained highly controversial and disturbing to a diverse range of professionals who had advocated its use as a therapeutic facilitator. This faction did not believe that Ecstasy should be freely available in the streets. These people did believe, however, that an appropriate categorization would be one that would enable further research as well as continued therapeutic use within controlled settings. Contrary to normal court proceedings by which "people are innocent until proven guilty," Ecstasy was actually viewed negatively and had to be proven innocent. This is often the case with various forms of drugs that are not seen in a "positive light" from the beginning. Also, since MDMA was reported to create great pleasure, it may have been very difficult to convince the government that this type of drug could also have redeeming therapeutic effects.[36] Such decisions are, however, supposed to be driven by written policies, science, and logic and not by politics or whim.

Since MDMA exerts salient sympathomimetic effects in its users, the possibility of performing a blind or double-blind design seems unrealistic. MDMA has central stimulant-like effects that are easily detectable by its users. Therefore, if an experimental design were to be performed, the experimental group—individuals receiving MDMA—would be keenly aware of being under the influence of this particular substance and be subject to bias in their responses. The acute sympathomimetic effects of MDMA (i.e., increased heartbeat, nausea, trismus) makes an objective design, at the very least, arduous.

If MDMA had been scientifically evaluated, it remains possible that this drug may have escaped from being categorized as a Schedule I drug. Although MDMA may have provided individuals with improved levels of functioning, the studies have not been scientifically carried out. Therefore, MDMA remains illegal and not permitted for use as a therapeutic adjunct or for use in general.

Chapter 4

MDMA and Drug-Assisted Psychotherapy

The empathic component, or degree of compatibility, is an essential aspect of psychotherapy. For therapy to be worthwhile, therapists must be able to establish some sort of rapport with their clients. Successful psychotherapy can be uniformly defined as the reaching of common mutual goals that have been set forth by both the therapist and client.

Most therapists guide clients based upon their own personal experiences, academic histories, and their very own common-sense wit. There always remain some barriers in that therapists, for the most part, are not actually able to wear the client's shoes or experience his or her hardships. Most professionals attempt to maintain objectivity to ensure that emotions don't override what is in the client's best interest. There are certain instances in which the therapist may have difficulty in thinking on the same level as the client. Since therapists are only human beings who have their own personal lives to live and own troubles to solve, it would not be possible or realistic for one to become emotionally or physically attached to each cancer or brain-injured patient, paraplegic, victim of incest, or drug addict. If therapists became emotionally involved with each of their incoming patients, they would most likely soon turn into clients themselves—as this would in time certainly take its toll.

Psychotherapy with or without drugs has been practiced as long as recorded history. Drug-assisted psychotherapy was believed to be a remedy in establishing immediate rapport and overcoming the existing communicational gaps between therapists and their clients. The psychotherapeutic utilization of substances during sessions drew initial enthusiasm; however, drug-assisted psychotherapeutic sessions are uncommon, or at least covert, nowadays.

The criticisms of such drug utilization included that there was insufficient data regarding the safety of particular substances and that no reports had yielded concrete support suggesting that substance-assisted psychotherapy was more efficacious than the mainstream approach. The opposing faction believed that the introduction of a substance within the scope of therapy could garner insights that would incredibly assist psychotherapists in helping their patients.

DRUG-ASSISTED PSYCHOTHERAPY

In the years preceding MDMA utilization, various other substances had been used within the offices of therapists to assist in the enhancing of the overall psychotherapeutic process. Sometimes just the client would be given a substance, while in other instances both the client and the therapist would ingest a particular substance. Substances were most often introduced into the realm of psychotherapy in an attempt to provide both parties with an open and communicative environment, with an alleged common level of understanding. There has always been ongoing dispute with regard to the actual therapeutic benefits that these drugs have on individuals. The administration of drugs for use within psychotherapy has run the full gamut of opinion, from unrelenting prohibition to passionate and indiscriminate acceptance.[1]

Many psychologists believe that the origins of most problems occur as a result of one's upbringing and particular developments in one's past. Thus, the common goal in psychoanalytic therapy is for the therapist to help interpret the client's past and then provide him or her with insight regarding both the meaning and impact of past occurrences, with hopes of bringing restrained memories to the foreground. This process is indeed a lengthy one, as the untangling of memories, interpretation, and follow-up guidance are all requisite aspects of the psychotherapeutic process.

Mind-penetrating compounds have been given to clients in an attempt to accelerate the entire psychoanalytic process. Particular substances were purported to have the ability to plunge quickly and deeply into one's past. It was the substance, in and of itself, that was being touted as breaking down ego defenses. The substance was purported to set the stage so that the therapist could gain quick access to an individual's past. The therapist's role was key throughout the session in the questioning, notetaking, and the overall conducting of the conversation. Substances were not believed to be a "truth serum" or "quick fix," but rather active catalysts in helping clients recall and express their earliest memories, including those formerly too painful to reveal. The therapist would carefully take note and then, along with the client, delicately take a backward mental stroll with the individual down roads rarely traveled.

The usefulness of psychotherapeutic agents has been recapitulated in various ways, but the most common forum taken by the advocates of psychotherapeutic catalysts appears to be summed up nicely in the following quotes:

> In the hallucinogenic experience, repressed memories flood forth in an emotional catharsis that leaves the once troubled individual liberated from the core trauma from which his/her psyche suffered.[2]
>
> Childhood memories are reactivated and relived with intense and extraordinary clarity accompanied by similar emotions. The flow of thoughts and feelings are so strong that they are difficult to repress.[3]

MDMA IN A THERAPEUTIC CONTEXT

During the late 1970s and early 1980s, MDMA was found on the shelves in the offices of several psychiatrists. MDMA was given to clients during therapeutic sessions, as it had been deemed to be a catalyst for facilitating communication and heightening recognition—or for the attaining of insight. This shimmering white powder, recognized by its nickname Ecstasy, was being touted as the chemical key to enlightenment. The drug was also thought of as possessing qualities that enhance both empathy and self-understanding.

The first publication with regard to the pharmacological action of MDMA was published in the latter part of 1970.[4] This report revealed that the substance elicits a controlled altered state, while also inducing feelings of sensuality or extreme gratification. The effective dosage when taken by humans was determined to be 75-150 mg when taken orally. Oral consumption is the primary means by which this substance is taken.

Some therapists believed that MDMA was a useful means for opening pathways of communication, as its use seemed to have helped individuals in their yearnings to lessen their inhibitions that may have otherwise created overall tension and discomfort.[5] In a detailed volume, one author reported numerous accounts in which people had taken MDMA with results that were allegedly beneficial, at least within a therapeutic setting.[6] She also describes several cases in which individuals had consumed MDMA for the purposes of both personal and spiritual growth.

Some professionals in the mental health field reported that the MDMA-induced state enabled people to resolve long-standing conflicts and interpersonal problems. Several of these accounts revealed that MDMA was a convenient way to help people reorganize their lives, hence helping people relinquish and deal with provoking memories, conflict, and anxiety that may have otherwise remained hidden at an unconscious level. Dr. George Greer, longtime MDMA advocate, reported that the substance enabled people to communicate ideas, beliefs, opinions, and memories that may have long been repressed.[7] A similar paper explained that MDMA-assisted therapy had been utilized as a means of gaining access to the very memories that may have otherwise remained confined.[8] The utilization of MDMA appears to have integrated components that include relaxation, spiritual achievement, and traditional methods of psychotherapy.

Dr. Joseph Downing, a medical doctor in favor of the administration of MDMA within therapy, described the drug's effects as being characterized by a sense of well-being in which patients are able to deal with childhood trauma or other deeply repressed emotions.[9] Prior to MDMA, other substances were similarly used within psychotherapy for the same purposes of recovering repressed material, particularly early childhood experiences.[1]

A variety of descriptions have been made with regard to MDMA; however, the use of MDMA within therapy seems to be summed up best in the following proclamation:

> MDMA encouraged the experience of emotions by reducing the fear response to perceived emotional threats. There were no direct observable harmful physical effects. For example, couples who were having marital problems were treated with MDMA-assisted psychotherapy by psychiatrists and psychotherapists who believed that MDMA could facilitate communication. Trauma victims were treated with MDMA-assisted psychotherapy to help them delve into the source[s] of their problems, experience a healing catharsis, and subsequently function more effectively.[10]

One report out of San Francisco described a female who had been abducted, assaulted, battered, and tortured by her assailants.[11] This individual, who described herself as "suicidal," showed little progress following intensive psychotherapy. Shortly thereafter, a psychiatrist in California decided to treat this person with MDMA. Following several MDMA-assisted sessions, this victim described the efficacy of MDMA as follows:

> I've taken it several times, and each time I felt a little less fearful. The drug helped me regain some measure of serenity and peace of mind and enabled me to begin living a normal life again. For the first time, I was able to face the experience, go back and piece together what had happened.[11]

Dr. Philip Wolfson had touted that MDMA had optimistic results when treating psychotic patients. MDMA was believed to be a "positive alternative" to the burdensome experiences and symptoms endured by individuals diagnosed as being psychotic. Dr. Wolfson found that:

> MDMA enhances social communication by reducing psychic defensiveness and by enabling an integration of conflicting personality elements into a cohesive sense of self. It is a drug that provides a centering experience, rather than an ego diffusing experience.[12]

It was not until the 1970s when therapists began administering the drug to facilitate the therapeutic process. (It was also during these years when people began using this drug on a recreational basis in search of a spiritual high.) Numerous anecdotal accounts have strongly suggested that MDMA is a valuable adjunct in therapeutic settings,[13] with minimal risks when its use is monitored.

In the first published clinical study, users reported to have experienced positive changes in attitudes or feelings.[14] This study was the only one to have been published with regard to the therapeutic utilization of MDMA. This investigation found that the MDMA-assisted psychotherapy was of help to most of the clients. Improved attitudes, better interpersonal relationships, and elevations in mood were common findings following MDMA sessions. These MDMA sessions took place between 1980 and

1983. All participants were carefully screened for existing medical conditions. Subjects were all given an MDMA dose of 75-150 mg and an additional subsequent dose of 50 or 75 mg as the effects of the drug began subsiding. The sympathomimetic effects reported included bruxism, trismus, nausea, blurred vision, and headache. Some of the subjects had been given a concomitant dose of propranolol or diazepam as a means of alleviating these acute sympathomimetic side effects.

The benefits that subjects reported while under the influence of MDMA were also investigated. All twenty-nine subjects described changes in their attitudes and their moods. The attitudinal changes included increased self-esteem, an acceptance of negative experiences, increased self-awareness, and becoming more open-minded. Other positive changes reported included relationship changes, belief changes, occupational changes, and spiritual changes. A follow-up analysis found that MDMA had been physically safe for all twenty-nine participants. The attending therapists of this study concluded that:

> Not only is communication enhanced during the session, but afterward as well. Once a therapeutically motivated person has experienced the lack of true risk involved in direct and open communication, it can be practiced without the assistance of MDMA. This ability can not only help resolve existing conflicts, but can also prevent future ones from occurring due to unexpressed fears or misunderstandings.[15]

Referring to the psychotherapeutic use of MDMA, another professional described the substance as useful in helping clients visit "emotionally charged memories."[16] Dozens of other reports have been documented, revealing the utility of MDMA as a means of spiritual attainment, self-exploration, and efficacy within the realm of therapy.[6] A similar report characterized MDMA as a useful compound for the establishing of mutual trust, while breaking down the inhibitions that may have otherwise taken a much more lengthy therapeutic plan.[17]

Dr. Downing performed a pilot study involving twenty-one participants.[18] The criterion for participation was to have already had at least one prior exposure to MDMA so that individuals would be able to have expectations going into the drug experience, somewhat decreasing the confounding role that "set" has on the drug experience. The subjects ingested between 0.8 to 1.9 mg/lb, with the mean dosage being 1.14 mg/lb. This is believed to be the approximate dosage typically taken on the streets.

The side effects reported were bruxism, headaches, and eyelid twitches. All subjects experienced an elevation in blood pressure and pulse rate, with the hypertensive effect peaking at about one hour following consumption. Most subjects reported positive mood changes, with no serious adverse effects. These findings support the notion that MDMA is reasonably safe when taken in low dosages and in controlled settings. These findings also demonstrate that MDMA elicits various bodily reactions in and of itself, without the influence of added environmental stimuli.

Dr. Richard Yensen, a clinical psychologist specializing in the administration and management of psychoactive drug use in psychotherapy, described MDMA as a compound that can be used rather safely when combined with psychotherapy and the accompanying additional procedures typically used for drug-assisted therapy.[19] Dr. Yensen also declared that MDMA had not fulfilled the necessary scientific criteria of double-blind methodology, but at the same time encouraged that these investigations be performed on MDMA to evaluate its apparent therapeutic usefulness. Dr. Richard Ingrasci, a psychiatrist accustomed to administering MDMA in private practice, admitted that MDMA is not a quick answer for therapy, but rather a catalyst for the entire therapeutic process.[20] This psychiatrist also suggested that "MDMA is like getting a glimpse of the picture on the box of a puzzle of life," and how individuals still need to put the pieces together.[21]

A fifty-seven-year-old woman described the value of MDMA in her life. This woman vividly described the overpowering impact that MDMA enabled her and her husband to experience, as her husband was nearing his death following a long-term bout with cancer. MDMA was described in the following manner:

> This drug can allow people to die well. They die well in the emotional arms of their families. They get reconciliation; they talk about things they normally would never talk about. . . . It's not particularly addictive, and even a one-shot deal would be marvelous for these people to go home after Uncle Joe dies and say, "Gee, I at least told him I loved him," and things like that. I think it's so sad that we don't have this in every hospital, not for just cancer patients, though I think it allows people to rise above their pain, too. . . . My husband died at home in his bed . . . But because the MDMA had opened his psychic door, I was able to put him in this deep, trance-like state so he was in great joy without the body.[22]

This MDMA experience, as conveyed by this woman, seems to reflect the position held by those who propose the administration of MDMA to dying patients. Regardless of how people view the consumption of illicit drugs, the description of MDMA by this woman is indeed an eye-opener in many ways.

Professionals, as well as some of the general population, have openly campaigned about the value of mind-altering substances for those suffering from illness and for those suffering pain on their deathbeds. Substance use for those who are suffering has long been discussed, considered, and debated.

CONCLUDING COMMENTS

Due to the prompt scheduling of MDMA, clinical studies involving the administration of MDMA have not been permitted. The continued investigations into the potential efficacy of MDMA were never carried out, as the drug was placed into a category that ultimately did not allow for any studies involving the employing of MDMA within a therapeutic setting.

There has been, however, a great deal written about the recreational use of Ecstasy, as this substance remains quite popular on the illicit drug market. It remains uncertain at this time if and to what extent MDMA would have been useful within the realm of therapy. It is noteworthy, however, that MDMA does indeed possess an additional property, perhaps more than therapeutic, which makes its use compelling.

Psychiatrists and a pharmacologist, affiliated with the University of California, were only recently given the first ever formal approval for MDMA administration in humans.[23] The United States Food and Drug Administration, Drug Enforcement Administration, and the California Research Advisory Panel all authorized the preliminary studies proposed by this research team. This was the first study done that included an experimental design with a control group used for comparative purposes. This experiment was the first ever to have incorporated a double-blind methodology and the employment of a placebo drug—an inactive substance. These researchers closely examined the psychobiological effects that MDMA induces.

It is uncertain at this time if more MDMA studies will be formally approved. MDMA remains illegal, with very strict penalties assessed for distribution, sale, and possession. The legal status of this compound and its continued underground manufacture makes it impossible to reveal the true efficacy that this substance may or may not have in hospital settings. Since the underground manufacturing of MDMA continues to soar, it remains unlikely that the DEA will ever even consider the use of this compound in a therapeutic context.

The introduction of any fast-acting substance within the scope of a psychotherapeutic session remains debatable. Even if MDMA and other substances provide individuals with increased "insight" and "self-understanding," many still find the administration of consciousness-altering substances to be inappropriate. For example, although alcohol is legal and known to decrease inhibitions and ease one's mind, the thought of a therapist and a client sipping wine or having a few beers during a session seems to be somewhat unbecoming to many mental health professionals.

Another issue brought to the forefront pertains to dissociation or state-dependent learning. This basically refers to the possibility that the information learned and troubling issues discussed during drug-assisted therapy may not be easily recalled after the effects of the drug have dissipated. The same may be conversely true in that information learned while drug-free may not be easily recollected while one is under the influence of a substance. It has been stated that in order for memory to exist, one's mind is required to be in a state that is "analogous" to that in which the impressions were first received.[24] Therefore, any positive insights attained during the course of substance therapy may be forgotten shortly afterward. Also, psychotropic agents may not necessarily help individuals recall truly repressed memories, but help conjure up fantasies. To assume that such fantasies are real would then, in fact, be detrimental and a hindrance to the therapeutic process as both the therapist and the patient would be working from a false common ground.

For those who have ever endured a physically painful illness or have observed a loved one slowly die in "agony," the idea of giving a loved one a mood-altering drug to enhance the last few weeks of one's life seems somewhat alluring. This is in no way suggesting that compounds such as MDMA be made perfectly legal and readily available for public use, but rather suggesting and perhaps recommending the administration of MDMA or similar acting compounds to individuals who have physically debilitating pain or a prognosis that includes steady and rapid deterioration with death expected within a specific time period.

Much has been written about the plight of terminally ill patients and the roles of both the medical staff and family member caregivers. The focus has been mostly on the needs of a dying patient including, yet not limited to, the control of pain and preservation of dignity or feelings of self-worth. To fulfill these major patient needs, many feel that psychoactive drugs should be introduced upon a request deemed to be mutual consent. With euthanasia and the "right to die movement" presently in the news, many have openly expressed their opinions regarding these and other highly debated issues surrounding terminal and increasingly painful illnesses.

Although psychoactive substances such as mescaline, marijuana, MDMA, and LSD may not be currently legal for use in medical settings, there does remain a possibility that such substances may one day be accepted, at least as an alternative to the more extreme actions being presently taken by those who have had unbearable pain and suffering (i.e., suicide, patient-assisted suicide). Action has been taken recently in California toward making marijuana legally available for individuals enduring terminal, painful, and debilitating conditions. The controversy regarding whether or not there is a legitimate place in our society for intoxication with substances this country shuns remains heated and ongoing.

Chapter 5

Music, Raves, and Ecstasy

ECSTASY IN RECREATIONAL SETTINGS

Since the early 1980s, Ecstasy has remained widely used on a recreational basis as a means of entertainment. Ecstasy continues to enjoy increasing popularity as individuals proceed to ingest this substance in bars and various nightclub settings, some of which are actually quite conducive to its use. This substance has steadily become the drug of choice for many weekend partiers in their late teens to middle and upper twenties. Presently, MDMA is one of the most popular of the illicit drugs, as its use continues to reach epidemic proportions in the United States, as well as in various other places worldwide.[1]

Most MDMA users report that the drug elicits feelings of love, euphoria, and sensuality. Ecstasy is typically taken at nightclubs, bars, cafés, and at increasingly popular "rave" events. Rave events and Ecstasy go hand in hand and are rarely seen without one another. Also, the terms rave and Ecstasy are mostly even used within the same sentence. Ecstasy has become more than just a drug. One writer described Ecstasy and the overall rave scene as "a way of life."[2]

THE RAVE HYSTERIA

In the middle part of the 1980s, a report was published within a popular lay-press magazine. The article described a drug known as "Ecstasy," a drug touted by some as a catalyst for healing (e.g., psychotherapeutic), and known to others as a fun drug used in recreational settings (e.g., clubs or bars). This report predicted that Ecstasy would prove to be just another curiosity which would soon pass in time:

> Given that Ecstasy isn't much of an aphrodisiac and doesn't pack the wallop of any number of other party drugs, it seems possible that it will be little more than a passing fad among "recreational" users—an ultimately disappointing street drug, something tried once because of all the hype and then discarded.[3]

Little did these authors know that Ecstasy would still be very much around a decade later and, moreover, a drug favorite among many young people. Furthermore, Ecstasy is the very drug responsible for the advent and ongoing surge of the increasingly popular rave events.

Raves are all-night dance parties in which people gather at a preplanned destination to explore a particular drug with each other. Although a rave can take place in almost any setting, raves have been most commonly reported to take place in clubs, empty warehouses, and in wide-open country fields.[4] These environments are often illuminated with laser lights and distinguished by the energizing music, which is for the most part dance inducing.

Surrounded by a colorful display of flickering strobe lights and propelled by techno music, people gather to explore this drug experience in a family-like manner, and as the attendees literally "March to the Beat of Ecstasy." Individuals at raves are commonly observed hugging, dancing, and moving to the pulsating lights and percussive music. MDMA has been inextricably linked to rave parties since the latter part of the 1980s and well into this decade. Although these events first took place in England, such planned festivities have since gained widespread popularity in the United States, particularly in major cities and on college campuses. Although Ecstasy is taken in various recreational arenas, raves have been the standard environment in which individuals are commonly under the influence of MDMA. One researcher drew an appropriate analogy regarding current MDMA use and its association with raves:

> If raves were considered an engine, then Ecstasy is the fuel which runs them.[5]

This statement seems to accurately reflect the rave movement, since Ecstasy seems to be the main ingredient at such venues. It is fair to assume that the rave scene would not have continued in such a burgeoning way without the presence of Ecstasy, and, conversely, Ecstasy would probably not have become so immensely popular without the rave scene. The link that these two have has become quite apparent.

Raves often attract some of the most enthusiastic individuals, including those who arrive wearing Ecstasy paraphernalia such as tall hats, shirts, and even pendants spelling out the word Ecstasy. While experiencing this drug trip, some also wear baseball caps with the letter "E" or "X." It is also common for rave attendees to be decked out in fluorescent T-shirts and have bandannas covering their heads.[6] Some attendees bring a pacifier to suck on, to avoid biting down on their inner cheeks and gums when grinding their teeth, a phenomenon known as bruxism, a troubling physical side effect of Ecstasy use.[7,8]

Most individuals who attend rave parties spend most of the time dancing to the lyricless tribal beats and bouncing around to the shattering sounds of both "techno" and "house," which are the main types of music that are played at such events.[9] These types of music supposedly began in Detroit and New York City respectively, but have quickly become popular worldwide.

It has been reported that the strobe lights, combined with the loud rhythmic beats, greatly contribute to the overall drug experience. Of course, the purity and frequency of MDMA use plays prominent in this and any other drug experience. Set and setting also vastly contribute to the excursion on Ecstasy, although it remains unconfirmed as to the exact role and impact these have during this particular drug experience. What is well known, however, is the fact that time has little meaning at these all-night and into the morning dance parties in which individuals hug, laugh, talk, scream, and dance on and on to the "Beat of Ecstasy." At rave events, the lights spin in a dizzying array of colors and shapes. Rave attendees consistently include people who are smiling, touching, dancing, and, for the most part, loving one another, with violence being the very last thing on their minds.[10]

Raves are held in hypnotic-like atmospheres in which the loud and repetitive music thrusts vibrations throughout the general environment and the attendees as well. The music has been described as "aesthetically hip," in essence creating an atmosphere that allegedly helps launch the Ecstasy experience to different heights. This is indeed a drug that has effects very much dependent upon the user, environment, music, and lighting. It would be fair to assume that MDMA use in quiet settings is much different than in louder ones. One individual described the significance that music has on the overall experience when saying "whoever it was who brought house music and Ecstasy together is a total genius, and I want to shake that man's hand."

Techno and house music have become very closely intertwined with the rave culture, as these musical patterns are believed to help generate what has been popularly described as being a "trance-induced" state. The music has been described as a pulsating musical engine, something likely to keep rave attendees very much "tuned in." The pounding sound of relentless music is said to radiate bass throughout one's body and soul. The sharp whistling sounds shrill at odds with the overall beat, creating further stimulation. Although such environments are body-penetrating in and of themselves, many individuals choose to add Ecstasy to the mix as a prized vehicle for imaginative transport.

Although rave events and Ecstasy use were formerly underground activities, these trends have continued in more open atmospheres, some of which have actually become renowned for Ecstasy distribution and use. Recently, a few clubs were closed down because of the alleged open use of Ecstasy upon the premises.[11] Nowadays, Ecstasy is taken by people of various socioeconomic backgrounds, diverse sexual orientations, and a wide range of educational backgrounds. Raves are described as a place of unity, a place for togetherness for all of those who are present.

It is noteworthy that most attendees do not just come to listen to music and dance. Most individuals bond and unite while under the influence of a mind-altering substance, indicating that raves are not just an environment for meeting people and dancing. While such venues may, indeed, be conducive for togetherness and conviviality, raves have become well known as havens for wide-open drug distribution and use.

Most young people who attend raves describe the atmosphere as "closely knit" and "family-like," with an overall strong sense of bonding. One rave attendee drew a popular response by many bystanders when she said:

> The rave scene is crazy, fun, dangerous—yet exciting. It's deadly. It's happening. It's all about how you dress and how you dance. It's about standing out and meeting people and just being able to live your youth.

There have been several individuals (e.g., parents) who envision raves in a much different light. Many feel that raves should be discontinued—or forbidden. Some of the more vocal individuals have included parents who have watched their own children fall victim to the rave scene and Ecstasy. The subsequent two chapters, Chapter 6 and Chapter 7, describe the impact that Ecstasy has had on families.

ECSTASY-RELATED STUDIES

A common generalization has been that the illegal drug market is mainly occupied by the less educated and poorer socioeconomic status populations. There have been instances in which our society was quick to judge and label drug users, such as when reports refer to users as "punks" or "junkies," insinuating that the people who take drugs are "losers" who have no other life purpose than to feed their brains with mind-altering drugs. In the past, some drug users and nondrug users were pointed out and immediately labeled because of their appearances. Individuals who use Ecstasy are not distinguishable by hairstyles, hygiene, or clothing as has been the case with other drugs in the past.[12] In the case of Ecstasy, there are no salient characteristics of the typical user. Ecstasy is believed to be particularly popular among college students and gay and lesbian populations. However, these individuals are not all Ecstasy users, and Ecstasy use is not limited to only these groups.

Ecstasy has been surfacing at many college campuses worldwide, including some of the most competitive schools. Interestingly, a study done out of one of the most respected universities in this country, Stanford University, revealed that nearly 40 percent of the undergraduates polled had taken Ecstasy on at least one occasion.[13] This study indicates that MDMA is not necessarily just taken by the common street person, but by individuals of high academic standings as well. Ecstasy has actually been labeled as the "chic" drug, as its use has continued to emerge at the high school level among the fairly well-educated and popular students.[14] A report published several years later revealed that MDMA use continues to increase among college students, as indicated by a short-term longitudinal study.[15] People continue to use this drug at parties and in other atmospheres conducive to its use. However, as was stated earlier, the environment that has been inextricably linked with Ecstasy is the rave party.[16] Increasing reports have suggested that some rave attendees take "candy flips"—the simultaneous consumption of both LSD and Ecstasy.[17,18]

Although questionnaire investigations and interviews provide valuable information, most often these studies are performed in a retrospective manner. An understanding of the MDMA experience—including the positive effects gained, the dosage, the set and setting, the sympathomimetic effects, and the list of adverse symptoms—remains incomplete. There have been several studies done, however, that have retrospectively analyzed the effects that users had encountered while under the influence and well after the use of MDMA.

A questionnaire was distributed to examine the effects that MDMA has on users.[8] This study involved a total of 100 subjects, whose frequency of use ranged from one to thirty-eight exposures. Most subjects reported feeling a sense of closeness with others shortly after ingesting the drug. Numerous sympathomimetic effects were reported to follow as well, including tachycardia, xerostomia, tremors, diaphoresis, heart palpitations, and both trismus and bruxism. This study also found that the pleasurable effects of the drug decreased with subsequent doses over a period of time.

Several years later, another research group made use of a detailed questionnaire to investigate the reports pertaining to the use of Ecstasy.[19] This study took place in Australia. The population sample consisted of 100 subjects, all of whom had admitted to taking Ecstasy on a recreational basis prior to being administered the questionnaire form. Many subjects did report feeling more sensual, open-minded, talkative, close with others, and euphoric. However, there were numerous subjects (50 percent) who also reported that Ecstasy had no effect whatsoever on their psychological state of mind, relationships, conviviality, or social interactions. Several did allude to having gained more insight while in the drug-induced state. Similar to other studies, this sample population of users did report experiencing a wide range of symptoms, including anorectic effects, xerostomia, tachycardia, and bruxism.

A retrospective investigation of Ecstasy among professionals was done to further examine the effects of MDMA.[20] This study consisted of twenty subjects with the criteria for participation being that subjects had to have at least one prior exposure to MDMA and be medical doctors. A semi-structured interview had been done individually with each of the twenty subjects. MDMA use in this particular sample ranged from a total of one to twenty-five lifetime exposures. The most common reports describing the effects of MDMA included altered time perception, increased conviviality and openness, decreased defensiveness, and an increased awareness of emotions. Several also reported that MDMA helped them become aware of previously unconscious memories. The documented adverse symptomatology were decreased appetite, trismus, bruxism, agitation, increased anxiety, and nausea, which resulted in vomiting among some users. The long-term benefits attributed to MDMA were improved social and interpersonal functioning, changes in life values, improved occupational functioning, and decreased defensiveness. This study depicted various psychological and behavioral phenomena associated with MDMA use, as well as adverse effects.

An archival study was done to analyze thirty-seven cases of individuals who had taken Ecstasy in Ireland.[21] This study investigated reports from a year-and-a-half time span. These reports were taken over the telephone by the Poisons Information Center in Dublin, Ireland. Data showed that most patients only had mild symptoms following Ecstasy consumption. The most common symptoms reported were agitation, heart palpitations, pupillary dilation, tachycardia, hypertension, CNS depression, and incontinence. This means of collecting data provides little, if any, information with regard to the positive effects associated with MDMA.

In the most recently published retrospective study, the subjective reports of hundreds of Ecstasy-using individuals were examined. This investigation employed a questionnaire that investigated the immediate bodily responses following ingestion, as well as the recurring side effects that manifest well after the drug experience.[7] This population sample consisted of a total of 500 participants. Findings revealed that individuals feel euphoric, more sexually aroused, and have noticeable increases in energy while under the influence of Ecstasy. This same study also investigated the drug-induced sympathomimetic effects of this substance. MDMA users experience lower backache, pupillary dilation, bruxism, nausea with and without actual vomiting, and sometimes, yet less often, depression and anxiety. Paranoia was also reported by a large number of participants. Recurring symptoms reported included derealization, headaches, lower backache, hypertonicity, flashbacks, depression, and insomnia. MDMA has been credited with a wide range of both physical and psychological manifestations, all of which will be discussed in the next chapter.

CONCLUDING COMMENTS

There has never been a drug that has been characterized in quite the same way as individuals describe Ecstasy. There have been drugs that have been depicted as making individuals feel "buzzed," "energetic," "alert," "mellow," "tired," and "high." In the case of Ecstasy, however, individuals have uniformly described its effects as "euphoric," "blissful," and love-inducing, qualities which make this drug distinct from other substances sold on either the licit or illicit market.

In the 1980s, when Ecstasy started to become rather popular, there was widespread belief that this substance was just a passing trend. The rave phenomenon and Ecstasy use, however, have proven to be anything but a fad or passing trend. As Ecstasy continues to be used with increasing popularity worldwide, there is no reason to believe that this drug or "rave" phenomenon will fade anytime soon from the recreational domain.

Throughout history, intoxication with various substances has become similar to the basic drives of hunger, thirst, and sex. The pursuit of the drug-induced state is not necessarily a biological need; it is more of a deeply embedded desire. Taking into account: (1) the euphoric effects that Ecstasy elicits; (2) individuals' desires to become intoxicated and explore their curiosity; and (3) the family-like atmosphere that raves supposedly provide, it seems likely that this substance shall be used for many years to come.

Although MDMA has been ascribed to many burdensome reactions, individuals continue to ingest Ecstasy and other street substances with little, or sometimes no, fear. Most who experiment with Ecstasy will remain unscathed in their pursuit; however, there shall be other individuals, unfortunately, who do not survive to even tell about their Ecstasy experiences. The upcoming chapters describe the discouraging, dangerous, and sometimes deadly side to Ecstasy.

Chapter 6

Adverse Reactions:
Beyond the Euphoric High

While one person can take a certain drug and have a pleasurable experience, another person may take the same drug and dosage at the same time in the same place and end up having irreversible side effects or perhaps a fatal reaction.[1] When it comes to different responses to drugs, psychological makeup is deemed to play a prominent role.

It has yet to be fully substantiated as to why just a handful of deaths occur among MDMA users, considering that millions of individuals continue to go to rave parties, and a good proportion of them are consuming Ecstasy.[2] This is by no means suggesting that this drug is safe. It is fortunate, yet surprising, that more deaths do not result as a consequence of MDMA intake, taking into account the wide array of implications that this drug has had on its users.

There have been a wide range of adverse effects and organic complications that have manifested shortly following recreational MDMA ingestion.

THE INITIAL EFFECTS OF ECSTASY

The effects of Ecstasy use, at least on a recreational basis, have been reported to be typically experienced or felt approximately twenty to forty minutes following ingestion, most often experienced as an "amphetamine-like rush."[3] Many Ecstasy users carefully time when they ingest the substance so that they will arrive at a club or rave approximately when the drug effects "kick in." Most users report that the drug is felt at or about thirty minutes following ingestion. It is at this time when people begin to feel increased heart rate, higher levels of energy, and sensations that are characterized as euphoric.

The initiatory psychological effects are often accompanied by sympathomimetic responses, typically manifesting in overt bodily responses. The sympathomimetic effects most frequently reported to occur at the onset of Ecstasy ingestion include pupillary dilation, lower backache, nausea, bruxism, tachycardia, headaches, vomiting, and blurred vision.[4,5] These autonomic bodily symptoms begin to manifest approximately thirty minutes following ingestion and usually continue with decreasing intensity throughout the entire six- to eight-hour drug experience. These acute sympathomimetic responses are typical in most users and, for the most part, dissipate with the passage of time. In some instances, however, individuals endure such a sudden and unexpected shock to their central nervous system that these physiological effects progress to more serious psychological manifestations and sometimes even organic complications.

Several review papers written within the literature have attempted to list the entire scope of residual symptoms that occur well after the MDMA experience.[6,7] Other MDMA-induced symptomatology have been documented in the form of individual letters to the editor and specific case reports. The manifesting reactions following Ecstasy use are included within Table 6.1.

PSYCHOLOGICAL SYMPTOMATOLOGY

A wide range of psychological side effects have been reported immediately upon MDMA ingestion, as well as long after the drug experience. MDMA-induced anxiety and transient episodes

TABLE 6.1. Symptomatology and Medical Complications Following MDMA Intake

Acute Reactions	Psychological Symptoms	Medical Complications
Pupillary dilation	Anxiety	Acute renal failure
Headache	Panic attacks	Intracranial hemorrhage
Hypertension	Disorientation	Convulsions/seizures
Nausea/vomiting	Psychosis	*DIC
Tachycardia	Depression	Rhabdomyolysis
Blurred vision	Delusions	Coma
Trismus/bruxism	Mood swings	Hepatitis
Hypertonicity	Catatonic stupor	Stroke
Lower backache	Depersonalization	Hyperthermia
Nystagmus	Derealization	Cerebral edema
Tremors	Insomnia	Aplastic anemia
Xerostomia	Lapses in memory	Jaundice
Diaphoresis	Flashbacks	Incontinence

*disseminated intravascular coagulation

of panic have been experienced following Ecstasy use.[8,9] One case described an individual who experienced panic that progressed to nausea, ataxia, vertigo, fear of imminent death, tachycardia, and hyperventilation. This subject was transported to the hospital and given diazepam intravenously and released shortly thereafter.[10] These cases included individuals who had no history of panic or anxiety attacks.

MDMA has also been reported to cause paranoia in its users,[11,12] with simultaneous feelings of depersonalization in some instances.[13] Paranoid ideations have been reported to occur concurrently with high levels of anxiety, delusions of bodily change, and extreme mood swings.[14] Reports have also indicated that MDMA users experience recurring flashbacks[15] characterized by concurrent depersonalization and paranoia.[16,17]

Numerous accounts of depression have been cited in the literature. One individual had presumably developed a major depressive disorder after having taken MDMA on several occasions.[18] This individual made a full recovery, but only after being prescribed a strict regimen of tricyclic antidepressant medications, including amitriptyline and tranylcypromine. Other reports have indicated that MDMA consumption either produced or exacerbated depressive symptomatology and, in some instances, had contributed to suicidal ideation.[11] Another case recapitulated the study of an individual who experienced depression that was characterized by lethargy, decreased appetite, hypersomnia, diminished ability to concentrate, and suicidal ideations.[19]

Although a true causal relation is unable to be drawn, several reports have indicated that MDMA intake precipitated cases of successful suicides shortly after its use.[20-23] A more recent report found a successful suicide to have been committed shortly following MDMA use.[24] This particular case ascribed MDMA as either directly triggering an impulsive short-term depressive episode or exacerbating a preexisting depressive disorder, resulting in suicide. Although it is arduous to determine a causal relation between MDMA use and depression/suicide, several indications have been demonstrated. Ongoing discussion continues with regard to whether psychological factors precipitate drug use, or if it is the drug that evokes the brain chemical changes that manifest in depressive symptomatology, and suicidal ideations in some instances.[25]

MDMA has been reported to evoke both immediate as well as prolonged adverse effects. Paranoid psychosis and psychotic episodes have been reported to manifest shortly following ingestion of MDMA, with some episodes known to manifest even well after the MDMA exposure.[12,14,17,26-28]

Recurring symptoms of panic attacks followed MDMA use in two individuals.[29] One subject endured repeat episodes that were characterized by classic symptoms of anxiety attacks, including shortness of breath, dizziness, nausea, tachycardia, trembling, and a feeling of impending doom. This subject also experienced depressive episodes leading to appetite loss and subsequent notable weight loss. The second case describes an individual who developed malingering neuropsychiatric manifestations following MDMA usage. This subject endured transient episodes of paranoia, anxiety, insomnia, memory disturbance, and depression. This person was treated with fluoxetine, and the various symptoms have discontinued. Although fluoxetine has been used successfully in treating individuals who develop brain chemical imbalances (i.e., serotonin), it is not advised that this medication be taken concurrently with MDMA as an antidote.[30] Although fluoxetine may indeed buffer some of the acute and aftereffects of Ecstasy, the medication does not protect one from adverse and toxic effects, considering that MDMA intake effects not only serotonin but other monoamines as well, including dopamine and norepinephrine.

MEDICAL COMPLICATIONS

MDMA-induced medical anomalies have been reported to occur shortly following ingestion. The mechanism of action of MDMA has yet to be fully delineated; however, convulsions, collapse, hyperthermia, rhabdomyolysis, disseminated intravascular coagulation, and acute renal failure have followed Ecstasy intake.[31] At rave events, the pharmacological effects of Ecstasy are believed to be compounded by physical exertion, hot and crowded atmospheres, and severe dehydration due to lack of fluid intake. It is therefore difficult to substantiate the exact roles that environmental and drug factors have in these presentations. Nonetheless, there has been a constellation of deleterious organic manifestations in response to MDMA ingestion.

MDMA-induced necrosis of the liver has been increasingly reported to occur following drug consumption.[32-34] Hepatitis has been reported to occur in MDMA users, including cases in which individuals were forced to have a liver transplant.[35] A recent work described eight patients who developed acute liver damage temporally related to Ecstasy consumption.[36] Four of these patients had such severe coagulopathy and encephalopathy that their conditions warranted a liver transplant. Of these patients, one survived after a successful transplantation, one died before a donor became available, and two patients died shortly following transplantation after enduring overwhelming sepsis. Another report recognized hepatitis as being a complication of MDMA use in three individuals, even though these subjects had minimum exposure to Ecstasy.[37] Another report described the onset of liver failure in a teenage female who had taken MDMA each weekend for the previous year.[38] This individual did recover after two months following her admission to a hospital.

Although there are many causes of anemia, one report found a temporal association between MDMA use and aplastic anemia.[39] This report described two individuals whose diagnoses were consistent with that of severe aplastic anemia in one subject and mild aplastic anemia in the other. Since bone marrow suppression was noted in these individuals, hematological monitoring is advised to those caring for individuals admitted following MDMA-induced anomalies.

Rhabdomyolysis has been reported to occur following MDMA ingestion. One case described an individual who had a convulsion, experienced urinary incontinence, and became increasingly restless following Ecstasy use.[40] This subject was treated with diazepam and chlorpromazine and intravenous hydration. This patient remained comatose for several hours after admission and then developed severe rhabdomyolysis. This subject recovered after five days of admission. Vigorous early treatment of rhabdomyolysis can prevent renal failure, another complication ascribed to MDMA use.[41,42] Another case of MDMA-induced rhabdomyolysis was found in a subject who presented unconscious with hyperthermia and convulsions.[43] This subject was successfully treated with thiopentine to control the seizures. Dantrolene was used with success in treating the MDMA-induced hyperthermia.

Dantrolene, although first marketed as a muscle relaxant, has been suggested as a remedy in response to hyperthermic reactions following MDMA use.[44] Other cases have been reported in which credence was given to dantrolene for helping restore normal body temperature following MDMA-induced hyperthermia. It has been pointed out that this medication, or any other, cannot be totally relied upon since MDMA-induced complications are progressive with many implications.

Several reports have found that individuals experience hyponatremia,[45,46] with some cases being characterized by catatonic stupor.[47] Catatonia has been described as episodes of abnormal motor behavior and periods of extreme hyperactivity or hypoactivity.[48] One case described two patients who were found to have cerebral edema following MDMA exposure. These individuals were found to have hyponatremia as well, with both making a full recovery a short time following treatment.[49] Some of these cases of induced hyponatremia may be caused by excessive fluid intake, often seen in MDMA users. Hydration is critical following MDMA use since fluids restore body perspiration lost as a consequence of the drug itself, as well as from physical exertion. However, excessive fluid intake can present a new range of complications, as has been observed in such cases of hyponatremia and cerebral edema.[50] It has been emphasized that water not be used as an antidote or safe means of prophylactics in preparation of the potential effects of MDMA.[51,52] MDMA induced a near-fatal hyponatremic reaction in one individual who had fallen unconscious and into a coma but was revived after vigorous treatment efforts.[53]

Intracerebral hemorrhage has also been reported to occur following recreational use of MDMA. One case reported an individual who entered the emergency department complaining of a severe headache that was accompanied by vomiting. Following a thorough clinical examination, a computed tomography (CT) scan was performed, thus revealing subarachnoid hemorrhaging.[54] Following treatment with nimodipine and a successful surgical procedure to deal with a drug-induced aneurysm, this subject made a complete recovery. Intracerebral hemorrhaging has been reported to occur in other MDMA users,[55] sometimes with fatal consequences.[56,57] Other cases have described isolated instances of cerebral infarction.[58] One case described an otherwise healthy man who had a sudden onset of a frontal headache with nausea and vomiting. Upon a neurological examination, it was determined that the subject had suffered a subcortical infarction, or stroke.[59] Although the mechanism of action leading to cerebral infarction is not able to be fully delineated, MDMA does potentiate serotonin, which is a neurotransmitter that serves as the most potent vasoconstrictor amine.[60] MDMA may have induced vasoconstriction of blood vessels, which not only led to a pronounced headache but ensuing stroke as well.

A most recent published report described the enduring impact that Ecstasy had upon a first-time user. A male in his late teens experienced a wide range of both short-term and long-term neuropsychiatric effects that caused manifold incapacitating conditions.[61] This individual reported to have endured an extensive cluster of residual symptoms, many of which appeared to have a psychiatric and neurological basis. The more salient manifestations that were described included, yet were not limited to, chronic headaches, blurred vision, anxiety, depression, lapses in memory, depersonalization, inappropriate pupil dilation, derealization, visceral sensations, déjà vu, sudden bursts of energy, and photosensitivity. It was also conveyed how this individual would drift into what were described as "trance-like" states.

After a complete physical examination, case assessment, blood work, and urinalysis, an electroencephalograph (EEG) and brain electrical activity mapping (BEAM) test were ordered to provide more concrete data of the occurrences within the temporal cortex of this patient. The findings yielded by the BEAM test, combined with the clinical assessment, were indicative of a neurological condition induced or at least exacerbated by the use of Ecstasy. Although it has yet to be fully substantiated, Ecstasy seems to have kindled the onset of temporal lobe epilepsy. The dual regimen of clonazepam and sertraline is the medication combination that ultimately ameliorated the many presenting effects that appeared following Ecstasy ingestion.

Although the reasons are unknown at this time, MDMA has been attributed to causing urinary incontinence in some users.[62] Since urinary incontinence is a common phenomenon following a stroke, its occurrence may serve as a indication that an individual has had a cerebral infarction.[63]

MDMA-induced cerebral venous sinus thrombosis has been reported in users, characterized by persistent migraine headaches.[64] MDMA-induced pneumomediastinum has been reported to occur in one user.[65] After vomiting for several hours following ingestion and experiencing chest pains, this subject was admitted to the emergency room. After a thorough examination, a clinical diagnosis of ruptured esophagus was made. Treatment included analgesia, intravenous fluids, and antibiotics. This subject made a complete recovery and has since remained asymptomatic.

MDMA-RELATED DEATHS

Although MDMA-related deaths have not been extensively documented, MDMA has been found to be implicated in several fatalities. One report, out of the office of the state medical examiner of New Jersey, originally stated that an individual had a "natural" death.[66] It was later determined, however, that MDMA ingestion occurred shortly prior to the subject's heart failure and death, as both the subject's blood and urinalysis identified only MDMA. Other reports of MDMA-induced deaths have also appeared within the literature.

As noted earlier, there has been relatively poor documentation with regard to human deaths related to MDMA use.[22] MDMA deaths have been deemed as atypical; however, this may be partly because the details of deaths go unreported.

Postmortem studies regarding deaths ascribed to MDMA intake have been performed.[67] These autopsies revealed striking changes in the liver, brain, and heart. Although hyperthermia is believed to account for MDMA-induced organic complications, hyperpyrexia was only noted in a few of these investigations. Hyperthermic reactions have been ascribed to various acute reactions including severe organic complications. Hyperthermia has been reported in a number of individuals who have been brought into casualty following MDMA intake. Hyperthermia has been diagnosed and treated successfully with dantrolene in some instances.[5,15,43,57,67] The postmortem study, however, suggests that MDMA-related deaths may occur even in the absence of hyperthermia.[68]

There have been cases which suggest that deaths can occur as a result of the effects of MDMA in and of itself, or as a result of the intoxicating effects of the drug that lead to altered perception and judgment. Cases of MDMA-related deaths have been associated with the operation of a vehicle, the climbing of an electrical utility tower, and sudden collapses following Ecstasy intake.[69,70] Since it is difficult to rule on the exact cause of deaths and implications of MDMA, one investigation used a tissue distribution to analyze two presumed drug-related deaths.[21] One cause of death was certified as a toxic reaction due to MDMA and alcohol. The second death was certified as a suicide in which MDMA had been taken a short time before the attempt. In another case, an individual was found dead in his home after presumably consuming Ecstasy. After a postmortem study, it was determined that this individual had body fluids containing several compounds, including MDMA.[71]

The most common sequence of complications leading to death includes fulminate hyperthermia, seizures, diaphoresis, tachycardia, disseminated intravascular coagulation, rhabdomyolysis, and renal failure.[72] MDMA complications were reported in a young man, who upon hospital admission was unconscious and sporadically convulsing.[73] Hyperthermia, tachycardia, and diaphoresis were noted. Within three hours following admission, disseminated intravascular coagulation was diagnosed with a prolonged clotting time. This patient's condition rapidly deteriorated, and he died within a short time.

The actions of MDMA remain unpredictable. One individual presented following Ecstasy use with agitation, hallucinations, diaphoresis, dilated pupils, tachycardia, nystagmus, and hyperthermia.[74] The hyperthermia was treated successfully with ice packs and moist towels. The medications, haloperidol and diazepam, were introduced into the realm of treatment. Laboratory evidence suggested rhabdomyolysis, coagulopathy, thrombocytopenia, delayed leukocytosis, and toxic hepatitis. This patient made a complete recovery. Others with similar complications, however, do not survive the MDMA experience and subsequent hospital treatment regimens. An individual was brought into casualty having hyperthermia, convulsions, pupillary dilation, and agitation.[75] This individual had ingested MDMA a short time prior to admission. The patient was deeply unconscious and, upon examination, was found to have cerebral edema. Although vigorous efforts were made to resuscitate this individual, this patient did die.

The complications of MDMA have been particularly prominent at "rave" dances. Although many instances of MDMA-induced disturbances and deaths are reported within the scientific literature, other reports are printed in the lay press for the reading convenience of the general community. One story sent shock waves across England when *The Sun* published a lengthy feature article along with a photo of a teenage girl who had recently fallen into a coma following Ecstasy use. The cover included a photo of the teenager fully attached to a life-support machine, with a big caption reading "Leah Took Ecstasy on Her 18th Birthday."[76] Although this case was the most salient to have ever appeared in the lay press, other cases have appeared as well.

An article appeared within the "Family Life" section of *The Times* in which a mother, using a pseudonym, describes the aftermath of the death of her son. This mother describes the subsequent hours after finding her teenage son dead in his bed, having supposedly suffered from heart failure following a night on Ecstasy.[77] Another report published within *The Times* describes and shows a photo of a teenage man who had fallen unconscious only to die shortly afterward.[78] The article quotes the young man's mother as saying that her son "hated drugs and called drug addicts and pushers the scum of the earth." This was believed to have been his first Ecstasy experience.

A barrage of articles continues to surface linking deaths to the increasingly popular "love drug" Ecstasy. Many MDMA-related deaths occur whereby individuals ingest the substance and later collapse, never to regain consciousness. One report described a teenage waterskiing champion who fell victim to the effects of Ecstasy.[79] Another report indicated that a teenage mechanic had become fatally ill following the recreational ingestion of Ecstasy.[80] An additional write-up focused on the pursuit of finding the dealers responsible for the selling of Ecstasy tablets.[81] The youngest person believed to have fallen victim to Ecstasy is a fifteen-year-old boy who, similar to others, took Ecstasy or "E" at a rave.[82] With the increasingly popular use of Ecstasy, along with the often glamorized rave parties, it is only a matter of time in which more cases of MDMA-related deaths appear in the lay-press and/or scientific literature.

CONCLUDING COMMENTS

Although some reports regarding the tragic effects of MDMA have ascribed physical exertion and dehydration to subsequent complications, many users who endure burdensome after-effects have not taken the drug in rave environments or participated in strenuous physical activity. Ecstasy has been linked to numerous cases in which users have endured deleterious reactions. These reported reactions have varied from manifesting side effects to organic complications that have been ultimately fatal in nature. The list of MDMA-related complications has continued to grow.

There has been some discussion within the literature with regard to the defining of adverse reactions following ingestion of various mind-altering compounds. Caution has been advised to those who write about or discuss adverse reactions that individuals endure following drug intake.[83] Some believe that the drug, in and of itself, induces various adverse consequences, while others believe that the use of drugs may exacerbate already established psychological or psychiatric conditions that may have otherwise not presented. Some users may actually be susceptible to adverse reactions if a psychological, psychiatric, or neurological abnormality already exists. It remains very possible that drugs alone may kindle the onset of a wide range of adverse consequences and/or exacerbate preexisting conditions (e.g., chemical imbalances).

What does remain certain, however, is that drugs taken on the illicit market are unpredictable and worthy of caution. For example, MDMA in its pure form can evoke transient side effects and even death. Moreover, drugs sold on the illicit market may be adulterated and not the drugs in their purest forms. One investigation with regard to MDMA found that, after having performed assays on dozens of tablets sold as Ecstasy, other ingredients were mixed in.[84]

Pharmacological studies indicate that MDMA produces central stimulant effects that appear to be mediated by the brain monoamines, serotonin and dopamine. Other cases seem to suggest that MDMA has its effects on serotonergic functioning, secondary to adrenergic activity. From the data published, it appears that MDMA is mediated by a combination of several neurotransmitter systems.

Set and setting have been considered to be integral factors regarding the overall drug experience, including the manifestation of adverse after-effects.[85] Set has been the term used to describe one's attitude and expectations prior to consuming a substance. The setting is characterized by physical surroundings, as well as the social situation. The exact implication that set and setting have with the onset of adverse reactions is unable to be determined at this time.

In the case of MDMA, all severe reactions have occurred in users who have taken the drug in unsupervised environments, which may imply significant environmental determinants. It must be noted that although environmental factors are legitimate, they do not counteract the very basic effects that MDMA has on neurotransmitter levels and serotonergic implications.

Cases have been described in which individuals developed complications that included hyperthermia, coma, hypertension, and marked agitation after they had consumed MDMA while under a regimen of monoamine oxidase inhibitors (MAOI).[86,87] Another case described an individual who collapsed and remained unconscious until his death five weeks later.[88] This individual had taken MDMA, amphetamine, and heroin the day before and an excessive amount of alcohol the day of his collapse. Concomitant use of MDMA and other substances including alcohol, LSD, amphetamines, heroin, and ketamine can indeed make the effects of MDMA synergistic and even more unpredictable. MDMA can produce manifestations by itself. However, when other drugs are taken simultaneously the drug actions may become complex and sometimes deadly. The simultaneous use of MDMA and prescribed medications may also pose problems.

This chapter serves as a reminder of the realistic dangers associated with illicit use of Ecstasy, including the devastating personal and biological manifestations that may proceed from ingestion. Extreme caution is advised to those who consider experimenting with the underground drug market, including the increasingly popular substance Ecstasy.

Chapter 7

The MDMA Experience:
Entering the World of Ecstasy

If one has never experimented with drugs, it is difficult for him or her to truly understand the drug-induced state. In no way is this suggesting or advising that one should go to a club and experiment with substances to truly understand the so-called "trip into the unknown." An alternative approach to understanding the Ecstasy-induced state is provided here, with a section designed to look deep into the world of Ecstasy.

This chapter makes several attempts to answer the commonly asked question: "What does it feel like to be on Ecstasy?" There is no way to completely describe the sensations that follow the ingestion of Ecstasy, or any other substance for that matter. Besides, describing the Ecstasy trip is a complex task because people report various feelings, bodily sensations, moods, sensitivities, and overall subjective experiences. It would be impossible to summarize the entire realm of Ecstasy-related experiences without gathering stories directly from several hundred individuals who have experimented with this substance. Therefore, in order for the successful completion of this chapter, several individuals who had prior exposure to Ecstasy were approached.

This chapter includes various descriptions of Ecstasy as told by several users. These narrations have been taken verbatim, both in writing and orally. For reasons of anonymity and in order to maintain the original agreement that was personally made with these individuals, there shall be no names listed with the following anecdotal accounts.

These excerpts may be of help to those wishing to either understand or further their understanding of the Ecstasy experience. Those who have already taken Ecstasy may find these quotes to be interesting and may, perhaps, be able to relate to some of these Ecstasy encounters. For those who have not taken Ecstasy, these reports may be either vicariously rewarding, simply informative, perhaps educational, and/or life-saving.

QUOTES STRAIGHT FROM USERS

Although many individuals agree that the setting and the company in which one takes the drug will have an effect on the drug experience, most report that the drug, in itself, creates feelings of happiness, conviviality, and love. The following quotes seem to represent the views most often expressed by the Ecstasy-using population:

- "Ecstasy is more or less a happy speed."
- "I felt feelings of complete happiness, content, and was more in touch with my feelings."
- "Ecstasy brings about ultimate pleasure. Your enemy is your friend."
- "Very intense. I felt as if nothing could be wrong or make me feel unhappy. Sometimes when I describe in detail my Ecstasy experiences, I start to have the feelings again."
- "Touching was wonderful. Kissing was great. I kissed someone I was in love with and almost felt like I was going to pass out from the intensity."
- "A very peaceful high. I felt very much in love with everyone around. It definitely lowered my inhibitions."
- "I felt happy and free and glad to be alive."
- "Out of control. Too much extra energy."
- "I became a walking and talking erogenous zone."
- "I was interested in everything in the most intense way. It is great stuff if you're in the right state of mind for it."

- "Ecstasy is like kissing someone for the first time and the kiss is everything you imagined it would be."
- "It was like being in a movie, in which I was the star."
- " . . . smiling and dancing, dancing and smiling. . . . "
- "This is not the type of drug to do alone. At the same time, it is best to be familiar and feel comfortable with the people you are with."
- "Ecstasy is sex, love, passion. It intensifies the most colorful aspects of life. The happiness it produces is temporary, maybe false, but I believe it opened my eyes to the most profound level of living."
- "It was like having the most fantastic four-hour orgasm."
- "All I wanted to do was smile. I was so wide awake, and I felt love for everything and everyone."
- "Pure energy. Happy energy. I felt tingly all over. It felt good to be touched. Being touched was so intense."
- "Ecstasy makes you feel very happy and energetic. I also think that if everyone were on Ecstasy there wouldn't be as many wars and conflicts in the world."
- "I felt utter bliss."
- "I felt like the world had changed into something very beautiful, which is much different from my usual views (very negative). On Ecstasy, happiness and beauty consume every thought, feeling, sensation, and desire."
- "I felt more social and more energetic. I also found myself being very self-aware."
- "I loved everything; life was beautiful. However, my back was insanely sore the last two times I did 'X.' I won't do it anymore for that reason."
- "It was like the feeling you have before ejaculating, but lasting two to three hours. I felt the need to be around people. They don't call it 'Ecstasy' for nothing. Don't do it alone!"
- "It is a benevolent feeling of connection with people, the community, the world, and your inner self."

- "It made me able to let my guard down and reveal my true self. I did experience mood fluctuations (ups and downs)."
- "It made the music I was listening to much more intense. I felt like I had a stereo inside my body."
- "I had a bad experience. I felt like I was surrounded by water and drowning. It must have been panic."
- "It was a lot of fun. You could kill your mother and enjoy it."
- "I recall being extremely happy. It changed my attitude about something that had been making me angry. My mind was at ease. I wish 'X' was around during my high school years."
- "I got a very enjoyable body buzz."
- "Ecstasy is the best drug ever, but the dangers keep me from frequently taking it. While on Ecstasy, I have bonded with people that I barely knew, many of whom will forever be my close friends."
- "I was excited to 'X' because I had heard so much about it. But nothing extraordinary happened. I may have been more talkative, but nothing special."
- "Floating, flying, highly sexual. I felt like I was on this really high mountain and I just wanted to stay there."
- "Feels like your blood is 115° Fahrenheit. You can feel the bass flow through your body like waves of kisses, accompanied by a sonic hug. Feels like your body is covered with sexually responsive skin. All bodily sensations are enhanced and pleasure filled."
- "Everyone was my friend. I don't think that anything could have brought me down. I loved it."
- "It made me think that life is just a dream. I had unbelievable sensations. I had extreme discomfort in my back. I probably wouldn't do it again."
- "Complete freedom of self-awareness, no inhibitions. A lot more prone to touching and feeling sexual. I was completely exhausted the next day. I got no sleep."

- "Everyone is your friend and the world seems to be in sync (which is not the case except when 'X-ing'). I don't crave it or need it, but I would do it again."
- "Wonderful . . . the best time of my life."
- "Breaks down the barriers that are formed when you're born."
- "It's an experience that must be tried."

The following account is a rather interesting one in that this individual was presumably under the influence of Ecstasy while writing this statement:

Life is beautiful; everything is great. I love my family and appreciate everything I have and ever had. I love life. I am happy and care about everybody's feelings. I love the people who are around me, because they are my friends. Is everyone as happy as me?—Or is it just me and the four other people who took Ecstasy an hour ago? Is this feeling of happiness real, or is it just from this pill? Am I really this happy, appreciative, and loving? I'll tell you tomorrow.

One user described the drug Ecstasy as follows:

Ecstasy is not a "happy drug." It, by itself, does not do anything. It does not contain any warmth, joy, wisdom, or experience. It contains a salt of millions of rather simple organic molecules—all identical. The Ecstasy and joy must come from within YOU. Ecstasy is a glimpse of the true empathy, calm wisdom, and energy you possess when you are living HERE and NOW and not based on the past. MDMA is a chemical key to the paradise within each of us. . . . I have seen the drug used responsibly to heal and purge the deep scars of childhood sexual abuse and uncoil deep-seated problems. In recent years, however, I have noticed the illicit MDMA scene to be burnt out, strung out, dishonest, and very unreliable. It has been a while since I have heard about the magic of Ecstasy heard commonly in the mid-1980s. All I seem to hear and see these days are sad and unbalanced individuals, mostly ravers, who are unable to integrate and link up the "neurosomatic vista" that Ecstasy allows for a glimpse of. These days, individuals take Ecstasy indiscriminately—sometimes taking mislabeled and adulterated tablets. The Ecstasy culture has changed.

These quotes are personal accounts of the ecstasy and/or rave experiences that people reported. Although most of these individuals described the drug in blissful ways, the drug has been known to induce long-lasting, sometimes even fatal, effects in users, as shall be described in the upcoming section.

WHEN TRAGEDY HITS HOME

One of the most difficult situations for a parent to encounter is having to bury his or her own child. It is a tragedy to have to lay away a child whether or not drugs were implicated in his or her death. There are, however, additional emotions that go hand in hand when a child dies following drug use. On one hand, some parents, close family members, and school personnel attempt to keep the cause of death quiet—and to some extent away from the grasp of society and the mass media. This may be mainly because individuals do not want to confront the possibility of being embarrassed by letting it become known that one's child and/or a particular school system may have been affiliated with drugs. Parents may also be guilt-ridden, perhaps believing that they may have been somewhat responsible for not properly raising or teaching their children.

At the other end of the spectrum, some parents are willing to openly deal with the death of their child, especially when there remains hope for helping to inform and save others from the same tragedy. Some individuals feel at least morally obligated to talk to the community about their son's or daughter's death so that potential drug users may reconsider whether they really want to risk their lives for a six- to eight-hour drug experience—a "trip" that one may ultimately not survive. Regardless, parents go through a grieving process that virtually lasts a lifetime.

It is easy to assume that a vast majority of Ecstasy users experience comfort, joy, love, conviviality, and euphoria—a feeling of well-being. It is also possible that individuals who have had bad reactions to Ecstasy may no longer hang out at bars, nightclubs, and rave events—and thus be unavailable to interview. Tragedies have, however, been voiced by several parents of those who have permanently fallen victim to Ecstasy.

Following the death of their daughter, one set of parents went on a crusade to reach out to the general public with hopes of deterring the epidemic use of Ecstasy in light of what the drug had recently done to their loved one.[1] These individuals talked publicly with reporters and at news conferences and appeared on widely televised syndicated talk shows. These individuals went so far as to release photographs of their coma-stricken daughter helplessly resting on life-support apparatus.[2] There was some controversy surrounding the publishing of these photos; however, these individuals were desperately attempting to dissuade others from taking this substance and perhaps ending up comatose in the same fetal-like position.

Others have also gone public regarding tragedies associated with the use of Ecstasy. An individual, in her late teens, appeared at a press conference with her parents shortly after she had awakened from an Ecstasy-induced coma.[3] This young lady, with assistance from both her parents, explained how this drug (Ecstasy) is not worth the "dance with death." Although this family appeared smiling in front of various media sources, the serious effects of Ecstasy were noticeable as the young woman was unable to speak above a whisper, due to a recently performed tracheotomy.

A tragic reaction following Ecstasy use was depicted in a letter written by a father who had recently buried his only child. The letter was electronically mailed onto a computer Web site. The letter reads as follows:

To whom this may concern,

My son, then a sophomore at UC Santa Cruz, died from the effects of Ecstasy (MDMA, Methylenedioxymethamphetamine) on April 1, 1995. He had gone to a rave in San Francisco at which he bought and ingested two Ecstasy tablets (about a half an hour apart), at about 4:30 a.m. He began to feel sick at the rave, and then returned to the house of a friend. He lost consciousness about 9:00 a.m. and was pronounced dead at the hospital at about 11:00 a.m.

There are lessons to be learned from his death.

You can die from a relatively low dose of Ecstasy. There were two autopsies performed. One attributed my son's death to "cardiac dysrhythmia due to an idiosyncratic drug reaction." The private pathologist attributed the death to "acute MDMA and alcohol intoxication."

MDMA has side effects short of death. My son had a prior bad experience with MDMA and was apparently worried about it. He sought information to help him decide whether to continue to take MDMA. He read articles and got a false sense of security about his continued MDMA use.

People should beware of immoderate or overly enthusiastic claims about the benefits of drugs and be skeptical of the claims made by MDMA promoters. Ask what any proponent of MDMA stands to gain from his or her advocacy. People should try to be sophisticated and mature in looking for the signs of addiction or dependence in themselves and in friends. Shortly after my son's passing, my wife and I found a truly nauseating collection of e-mails about his death. Their gist was either that the news was false, or that his death must have been an aberration due to some carelessness on his part. It was neither. He did die. He was no more careless than tens of thousands of other young people who take MDMA regularly. He just died. The drug killed him. The truth about drugs is that they are to be avoided not because they are sinister, but because their attractions come with awful risks of death, injury, disability, or other permanent suffering.

I hope you, the reader, will take some extra effort to be sure that you come to a well-informed, considerate, and personal evaluation of just how (or whether) recreational drugs should fit into this life.

Sadly Yours

FINAL WORDS ON ECSTASY

It has been anecdotally explained that MDMA users must drink "plenty" of fluids. It is indeed important that individuals maintain fluid intake to prevent dehydration and its related symptoms. However, an entire new realm of complications may arise upon rapid fluid intake within a short time since kidney function has been known in some instances to literally "shutdown."[4] Ecstasy has been thought to also stimulate an antidiuretic hormone, which after intake of rather excessive quantities of water may prove dangerous.[5] Ideally, individuals should drink in moderation or slowly throughout the excursion on Ecstasy, as opposed to overindulging on fluids upon feeling thirsty.

Ecstasy shall continue to be taken in various settings regardless of any detrimental message, that is unless one's close friend or fellow community member has a dreadful reaction from its use. Although there are some pamphlets and guides printed to help the user experience the most beneficial or supposedly safe trip while doing Ecstasy, there have been other reports regarding the individuals who may be at particular risk of experiencing burdensome aftereffects.

It has been documented that individuals who are most susceptible to prolonged or perhaps fatal consequences after Ecstasy ingestion are those who have had a history of heart problems, high blood pressure, depression, behavioral outbursts, and panic attacks. It has also been suggested that individuals avoid the use of Ecstasy if they have asthma, hypoglycemia, diabetes, epilepsy, a mood disorder, an irregular heartbeat, or an eating disorder.[6] Although certain conditions have been labeled as making one more vulnerable to the side effects of the Ecstasy trip, realistically speaking—every user is taking a risk when he or she ingests Ecstasy. Taking Ecstasy, as with any other drug sold on the illicit market, is similar to playing "Russian roulette," and its use should be carefully considered.

Chapter 8

Society, Drug Use, and Ecstasy

Everyone has his or her own perspective on drug use and the role that society should play these days while drugs are reaching epidemic proportions. Some believe that drugs are simply "dangerous," "evil," "unhealthy," and "wrong," with nothing more needed to be said. On the other hand, there are those individuals who feel that the use of drugs (legal or illegal) in moderation is alright. These attitudinal differences have been in existence since antiquity, with opinions ranging far and wide in both directions.

In an extensive article written for a periodical in England, the author agreed that Ecstasy is being consumed by hundreds of thousands of individuals each weekend, but felt that there is a moral responsibility to inform the users of the potential dangers associated with Ecstasy so that the users can take precautionary measures.[1] Although it is not advised that people use such drugs as marijuana, alcohol, LSD, or Ecstasy, these substances are bound to remain drugs of choice throughout the world regardless of any particular message that is being broadcasted. It has gotten to the point where individuals must not only be informed about particular dangers, but also, perhaps, learn more about actually putting this knowledge to use in what is today referred to as "self-efficacy." A perfect example of this is the fact that individuals continue to smoke cigarettes despite knowing the strong degree of association between smoking and cancer. Moreover, weight lifters continue to inject themselves with steroids, even though various complications have been known to be attributed to these substances.

MIXED MESSAGES

There are a variety of mixed messages conveyed by society and the mass media at large. Whether the message is simply untrue or perfectly reasonable, individuals seem to have become desensitized to the words written in the lay press or spoken on the television. Individuals do not know what to believe, who to believe, or if they should even bother to pay attention any longer.

It is noteworthy that society focuses a great deal of compelling attention on the drugs that are consumed on the illicit market. In many ways, there are a variety of covert mixed messages being broadcasted when there are sounds of alarm ringing with regard to the use of illegal drugs, considering that many injuries and deaths continue to be reported following the use of legal substances, mainly alcohol. The paradoxical message being communicated through the mass media is voiced through slogans such as "Just Say No" or "Just Don't Do It." While these mottos have become well-known nationwide, the same mass media of communication also broadcasts the commercials and billboards that contain advertisements for some of the most addictive, dangerous, and lethal substances. These substances happen to be uncontrolled and even sometimes readily available at one's local convenience store (e.g., tobacco, alcohol, caffeine).[2]

It is perplexing that alcohol remains perfectly legal and readily available within environments actually conducive to its use. In 1970, the Controlled Substances Act (CSA) was passed in order to put control on those particular substances deemed to have a potential for abuse. The CSA contains five separate categories, Schedule I-Schedule V, each indicating the restrictions on how or even if drugs are to be utilized. Schedule I contains substances thought to have a high potential for abuse, with no acceptable medical use. The other categories list those drugs that have been placed under control, with the degree of restriction decreasing with each subsequent scheduling category.

Alcohol has not been placed under the control of any of the schedules of the CSA; however, alcohol is very much an abused substance. Moreover, the only restrictions regarding the consumption of alcohol are that individuals must be a certain age, most often twenty-one, and maintain a blood alcohol level below a certain percentage if one is to drive a vehicle. Many physicians, psychologists, nurses, and medical personnel mutually agree that alcohol is an abused substance. It is also well known that alcohol has been attributed to various illnesses, motor vehicle accidents, and millions of deaths worldwide. Although these are commonly accepted facts, alcohol remains legal, with no controlled enforcement.

Alcohol manufacture and use is presumably still permissible because of the public outrage when strides were taken toward prohibition. This is paradoxical in itself, being that alcohol continues to be associated with violence and aggressive acts after consumption. Other puzzling messages have come in the form of slogans regarding alcohol consumption, including "Don't Drink and Drive" and "Stay Alive—Don't Drink and Drive." While these messages are indeed good ones, nearly all bars continue to have parking lots just outside their doors. This is very ironic! It is understandable that individuals should be responsible enough to not drive after drinking alcohol; however, it must be reiterated that alcoholism is an illness, in which many times people drink alone and do not have that "designated driver" available every time they have the urge to drink.

Since alcohol has been attributed to a voluminous amount of catastrophes and deaths, one can only ask oneself why this substance remains freely shelved in stores with no restrictions. Advocates of Ecstasy remain baffled that MDMA had been urgently banned in the 1980s, considering that there had been no confirmed deaths attributed to this substance. There continues to be great controversy surrounding the sudden prohibition of Ecstasy, especially since alcohol is the drug that has and will continue to be ascribed to hundreds of thousands of deaths annually. And although two wrongs don't make a right, there continues to be ongoing debate regarding the legislation of Ecstasy and a need for consistency in drug laws.

A substantial amount of attention has recently been focused upon the legalization of marijuana for medicinal use. This substance has been touted as being medically useful for individuals enduring pain from diseases including cancer and glaucoma. Individuals, who have not had a history of using mind-altering substances, have admitted to being introduced to such drugs as marijuana and Ecstasy in their desperate attempts to soothe the burdensome symptoms that have incapacitated them during their illnesses. Although marijuana may indeed produce effects that alleviate pain and suffering, the government has been known to disregard such possibilities.

At the present time, it is difficult to predict if and when particular substances may become legalized again. While this country does not seem to mind if people alter their state of consciousness, there does remain a power struggle with regard to how people choose to do so. The common trend, as far as the legal history of substances is concerned, seems to be that the better a certain drug makes one feel, the more apt that the substance is to be banned. The legal system and society at large have conveyed mixed messages; however, it must be reiterated that recreational drug use on the clandestine market is unpredictable, erratic, risky, and perhaps deadly.

Appendix

STATE AGENCIES FOR THE PREVENTION AND TREATMENT OF DRUG ABUSE

Alabama

Division of Substance Abuse Services
Alabama Department of Mental Health
RSA Union Building
100 N. Union Street
Montgomery, Alabama 36130-1410

Alaska

Division of Alcoholism and Drug Abuse
Alaska Department of Health and Human Services
240 Main Street, Suite 701
Juneau, Alaska 99811

Arizona

Office of Substance Abuse
Division of Behavioral Services
Arizona Department of Health Services
2122 East Highland
Phoenix, Arizona 85016

Arkansas

Arkansas Bureau of Alcohol and Drug Abuse Prevention
5800 West 10th Street, Suite 907
Little Rock, Arkansas 72204

California

Department of Alcohol and Drug Programs
California Health and Welfare Agency
1700 K Street, Fifth Floor
Sacramento, California 95814-4037

Colorado

Alcohol and Drug Abuse Division
Colorado Department of Human Services
4300 Cherry Creek Drive, South
Denver, Colorado 80222-1530

Connecticut

Department of Mental Health and Addiction Services
410 Capitol Avenue, MS 14COM
Hartford, Connecticut 06134

Delaware

Delaware Health and Social Services
Division of Alcoholism, Drug Abuse, and Mental Health
1901 North Dupont Highway
New Castle, Delaware 19720

District of Columbia

Addiction, Prevention and Recovery
1300 First Street, NE, Suite 300
Washington, DC 20002

Florida

Florida Department of Children and Families
Substance Abuse Programs
1317 Winewood Boulevard
Building 3, Room 101Y
Tallahassee, Florida 32399-0700

Georgia

Division of Mental Health
Georgia Department of Human Resources
2 Peachtree Street, NW
Atlanta, Georgia 30303-3171

Hawaii

Alcohol and Drug Abuse Division
Hawaii Department of Health
1270 Queen Emma Street, Suite 305
Honolulu, Hawaii 96813

Idaho

Bureau of Mental Health and Substance Abuse Services
Division of Family and Community Services
Idaho Department of Health and Welfare
450 West State Street
Boise, Idaho 83720

Illinois

Illinois Department of Alcoholism and Substance Abuse
James R. Thompson Center
100 West Randolph Street, Suite 5-600
Chicago, Illinois 60601

Indiana

Bureau of Addiction Services
Division of Mental Health
Indiana Family Services and Social Services Administration
402 West Washington Street, Room W-353
Indianapolis, Indiana 46204-2739

Iowa

Division of Substance Abuse and Health Promotion
Iowa Department of Public Health
321 East 12th Street
Lucas State Office Building, Third Floor
Des Moines, Iowa 50319-0075

Kansas

Alcohol and Drug Abuse Services
Department of Social and Rehabilitation Services
300 SW Oakley, Biddle Building
Topeka, Kansas 66606-1861

Kentucky

Division of Substance Abuse
Kentucky Department of Mental Health and Mental Retardation
275 East Main Street
Frankfort, Kentucky 40621

Louisiana

Office of Alcohol and Drug Abuse
Louisiana Department of Health
P.O. Box 2790, BIN # 18
Baton Rouge, Louisiana 70821-3868

Maine

Maine Office of Substance Abuse
Augusta Mental Health Complex
Marquardt Building, Third Floor
159 State House Station
Augusta, Maine 04333-0159

Maryland

Alcohol and Drug Abuse Services
Maryland Department of Health and Mental Hygiene
201 West Preston Street, 4th Floor
Baltimore, Maryland 21201

Massachusetts

Bureau of Substance Abuse
Massachusetts Department of Public Health
250 Washington Street
Boston, Massachusetts 02108

Michigan

Center for Substance Abuse Services
Michigan Department of Community Health
P.O. Box 30195
Lansing, Michigan 48909

Minnesota

Chemical Dependency Program Division
Minnesota Department of Human Services
444 Lafayette Road, North
St. Paul, Minnesota 55155-3823

Mississippi

Division of Alcohol and Drug Abuse
Mississippi Department of Mental Health
Robert E. Lee State Building
239 North Lamar Street, 11th Floor
Jackson, Mississippi 39201

Missouri

Division of Alcohol and Drug Abuse
Missouri Department of Mental Health
P.O. Box 687
Jefferson City, Missouri 65102-0687

Montana

Department of Health and Human Services
Addictive and Mental Disorders Division
P.O. Box 202951
Helena, Montana 59620-2951

Nebraska

Division of Alcoholism, Drug Abuse and Addiction Services
Nebraska Department of Health
P.O. Box 94728
Lincoln, Nebraska 68509-4728

Nevada

Bureau of Alcohol and Drug Abuse
505 East King Street, Room 500
Carson City, Nevada 89710

New Hampshire

Office of Alcohol and Drug Abuse Prevention
New Hampshire Department of Health and Human Services
105 Pleasant Street
Concord, New Hampshire 03301

New Jersey

Division of Alcoholism, Drug Abuse and Addiction Services
New Jersey Department of Health
CN 362
Trenton, New Jersey 08625-0362

New Mexico

Behavioral Health Services
New Mexico Department of Health
Harold Runnels Building, Room 3200
1190 St. Francis Street
Santa Fe, New Mexico 87501

New York

New York Office of Alcoholism and Substance Abuse Services
1450 Western Avenue
Albany, New York 12203-3526

North Carolina

North Carolina Department of Health and Human Services
Substance Abuse Services Section
325 North Salisbury Street
Raleigh, North Carolina 27603

North Dakota

North Dakota Department of Human Services
Division of Mental Health and Substance Abuse Services
600 South 2nd Street, Suite #1F
Bismarck, North Dakota 58504-8920

Ohio

Ohio Department of Alcohol and Drug Addiction Services
280 North High Street
Two Nationwide Plaza, 12th Floor
Columbus, Ohio 43215-2537

Oklahoma

Oklahoma Department of Mental Health
and Substance Abuse Services
P.O. Box 53277, Capitol Station
Oklahoma City, Oklahoma 73152

Oregon

Oregon Department of Human Services
Office of Alcohol and Drug Abuse Programs
Human Resources Building, Third Floor
500 Summer Street, NE
Salem, Oregon 97310-1016

Pennsylvania

Pennsylvania Department of Health
Office of Drug and Alcohol Programs
P.O. Box 90, Room 933
Harrisburg, Pennsylvania 17108

Rhode Island

Rhode Island Department of Health
Division of Substance Abuse
Cannon Building, Suite 105
3 Capitol Hill
Providence, Rhode Island 02908-5097

South Carolina

South Carolina Department of Alcohol
and Other Drug Abuse Services
3700 Forest Drive, Suite 300
Columbia, South Carolina 29204-4082

South Dakota

Division of Alcohol and Drug Abuse
South Dakota Department of Health and Human Services
Hillsview Plaza, East Highway 34
Pierre, South Dakota 57501-5070

Tennessee

Bureau of Substance Abuse
Services Division
Tennessee Department of Health
Cordell Hull Building, 3rd Floor
426 Fifth Avenue, North
Nashville, Tennessee 37247-4401

Texas

Texas Commission on Alcohol and Drug Abuse
9001 North IH 35
Austin, Texas 78753-5233

Utah

Division of Substance Abuse
Utah Department of Human Services
120 North 200 West, Room 413
Salt Lake City, Utah 84103

Vermont

Office of Alcohol and Drug Abuse
Vermont Agency of Human Services
108 Cherry Street
Burlington, Vermont 05402

Virginia

Office of Substance Abuse Services
Virginia Department of Mental Health
P.O. Box 1797
Richmond, Virginia 23214

Washington

Division of Alcohol and Substance Abuse
Washington Department of Social and Health Services
P.O. Box 45330
Olympia, Washington 98504-5330

West Virginia

Division of Alcohol and Drug Abuse
Office of Behavioral Health Services
West Virginia Department of Health
1900 Kanawha Boulevard
Capitol Complex, Building 6, Room 738
Charleston, West Virginia 25305

Wisconsin

Bureau of Substance Abuse Services
Department of Health and Family Services
P.O. Box 7851
Madison, Wisconsin 53707-7851

Wyoming

Division of Behavioral Health
Department of Health
447 Hathaway Building
Cheyenne, Wyoming 82002

Notes

Chapter 1

1. Rodgers, J. Foreword, In the mainstream of American life. In S.H. Snyder (Ed.), *The Encyclopedia of Psychoactive Drugs.* New York: Chelsea House, 1988.

2. Towers, A. *Student Drug and Alcohol Abuse: How Schools Can Help.* Washington, DC Combat Series (Eric Document Reproduction Service No. ED-284098). Washington, DC: U.S. Department of Education, 1989.

3. Kandel, D.B. and Yamaguchi, K. Developmental patterns of legal, illegal, and medically prescribed psychotropic drugs from adolescence to young adulthood. In C.L. Jones and R.J. Bates (Eds.), *Etiology of Drug Abuse: Implications for Prevention* (DHHS Publication No. [ADM] [85-01335). Washington, DC: U.S. Government Printing Office, 1985.

4. Bratter, T.E. The drug mystique. In R.C. Kolodny, T.E. Bratter, and C. Deep (Eds.), *Surviving Your Adolescent's Adolescence.* Boston, MA: Little Brown, 1984.

5. Tyler, A. *Street Drugs*, London: Hodder and Stoughton, 1995.

6. Kaplan, L.S. *Coping with Peer Pressure.* New York: Rosen Publishing Group, 1995.

7. Johnston, L.D., O'Malley, P.M., and Bachman, J.G. *Use of Licit and Illicit Drugs by America's High School Students (1975-1985).* Ann Arbor, MI: The University Institute for Social Research, 1985.

8. Wallack, L. and Corbett K. Illicit drug, tobacco, and alcohol use among youth: Trends and promising approaches in prevention. In H. Resnick (Ed.), *Youth and Drugs: Society's Mixed Messages.* OSAP Prevention Monograph 6, (DHHS Publication No. [ADM] (90-1689). Rockville, MD: U.S. Department of Health and Human Services, 1990.

9. Weil, A. and Rosen, W. *From Chocolate to Morphine.* Boston, MA: Houghton Mifflin, 1993.

10. Peroutka, S.J. Incidence of recreational use of 3,4-methylenedioxymethamphetamine (MDMA; "Ecstasy") on an undergraduate campus. *New England Journal of Medicine*, 1987, 317:1542-1543.

11. Solowij, N., Hall, W., and Lee, N. Recreational MDMA use in Sydney: A profile of "Ecstasy" users and their experiences with the drug. *British Journal of Addictions*, 1992, 87:1161-1172.

12. Cuomo, M.J., Dyment, P.G., and Gammino, V.M. Increasing use of "Ecstasy" (MDMA) and other hallucinogens on a college campus. *Journal of American College Health*, 1994, 42:271-274.

13. Cohen, R.S. Subjective reports on the effects of the MDMA ("Ecstasy") experience in humans. *Progress in Neuro-Psychopharmacology and Biological Psychiatry*, 1995, 19:1137-1145.

14. Ray, O. and Ksir, C. *Drugs, Society, and Human Behavior.* St. Louis, MO: Mosby, 1993.

15. Arkin, E.B. and Funkhouser, J.E. (Eds.). *Communicating about Alcohol and Other Drugs: Strategies for Reaching Populations at Risk.* OSAP Prevention Monograph 5, (DHHS Publication No. [ADM] (92-1665). Washington, DC: U.S. Department of Health and Human Services, 1992.

16. Beck, J. and Rosenbaum, M. *Pursuit of Ecstasy: The MDMA Experience.* New York: SUNY Press, 1994.

17. Patentschrift. *Verfahren zur Darstellung von Alkyloxyaryl-, Dialkyloxyaryl-, und Alkylenedioxy-arylaminopropanen bzw. deren am Stickstoff monoalkylierten Derivaten.* Firma E. Merck in Darmstadt, Germany, 1914.

18. Liester, M.B., Grob, C.S., Bravo, G.L., and Walsh, R.N. Phenomenology and sequelae of 3,4-methylenedioxymethamphetamine use. *Journal of Nervous and Mental Disease*, 1992, 180:345-352.

19. Merck, E. Formyl derivatives of secondary bases. German Patent No. 334,555. *Chemical Abstracts*, 1923, 17:1803-1804.

20. Hardman, H.F., Haavik, C.O., and Seevers, M.H. Relationship of the structure of mescaline and seven analogs to toxicity and behavior in five species of laboratory animals. *Toxicology and Applied Pharmacology*, 1973, 25:299-309.

21. Ricaurte, G.A., Bryan, G., Strauss, L., Seiden, L., and Schuster, L. Hallucinogenic amphetamine selectively destroys brain serotonin nerve terminals. *Science*, 1985, 229:986-988.

22. Seymour, R.B. *MDMA.* San Francisco, CA: Haight Ashbury Press, 1986.

23. Gaston, T.R. and Rasmussen, G.T. Identification of 3,4-methylenedioxymethamphetamine. *Microgram*, 1972, 5:60-63.

24. Sreenivasan, V.R. Problems in identification of methylenedioxy and methoxy amphetamines. *The Journal of Criminal Law, Criminology and Police Science*, 1972, 63:304-312.

25. Eichmeier, L.S. and Caplis, M.E. The forensic chemist: An "analytical detective." *Analytical Chemistry*, 1975, 47:841A-844A.

26. Shulgin, A.T. History of MDMA. In S.J. Peroutka (Ed.), *Ecstasy: The Clinical, Pharmacological, and Neurotoxicological Effects of the Drug MDMA.* Boston, MA: Kluwer Academic Publishers, 1990.

27. Adamson, S. *Through the Gateway of the Heart: Accounts of Experiences with MDMA and Other Empathogenic Substances.* San Francisco, CA: Four Trees Publications, 1985.

28. Gallagher, W. MDMA: Is there ever a justifiable reason for getting high? *Discover*, 1986, 7:34.

29. Siegel, R.K. Chemical Ecstasies. *Omni*, 1985, 8:29.

30. Abramson, D.M. The new drug underground. *New Age*, 1985, 10:35-40.

31. Ecstasy: Everything looks wonderful when you're young and on drugs. *Wet Magazine*, 1981, 9:76.

32. Dowling, C.G. The trouble with Ecstasy. *Life Magazine*, 1985, 8:88-94.

33. Gertz, K.R. "Hug Drug" alert: The agony of Ecstasy. *Harpers Bazaar*, 1985, 119:48,46,263.

34. Randall, T. "Rave" scene, Ecstasy use, leap Atlantic. *Journal of the American Medical Association*, 1992, 268:1506.

35. McDowell, D. Ecstasy and raves: The '90s party scene. In M.W. Fischman (Chair), *Hallucinogens, LSD, and Raves*. Washington, DC: Symposium conducted at the National Press Club, November 1993.

36. Neufeld, V. (Executive Producer). *20/20*. New York: WABC, January 24, 1997.

Chapter 2

1. Shulgin, A.T. What is MDMA? *Pharmchem Newsletter*, 1985, 14:3-5,10-11.

2. Saunders, N. *E for Ecstasy*. London: Neal's Yard Desktop Publishing, 1993.

3. Patentschrift. *Verfahren zur Darstellung von Alkyloxyaryl-, Dialkyloxyaryl- und Alkylenedioxy-arylaminopropanen bzw. deren am Stickstoff monoalkylierten Derivaten*. Firma E. Merck in Darmstadt, Germany, 1914.

4. Kirsch, M. M. *Designer Drugs*. Minneapolis, MN: Compcare, 1986, p. 1.

5. McCormick, M. *Designer Drug Abuse*. New York: Franklin Watts, 1989.

6. Beck, J. and Morgan, P.A. Designer drug confusion: A focus on MDMA. *Journal of Drug Education*, 1986, 16:287-302.

7. Riedlinger, T. and Riedlinger, J. The "seven deadly sins" of media hype in light of the MDMA controversy. In T. Lyttle (Ed.), *Psychedelic Monographs and Essays*. Boynton Beach, FL: PM&E Publishing Group, 1989.

8. Production process eliminates MDMA's psychedelic properties biochemist says. *Brain/Mind Bulletin*, April 15, 1985, 10:1-4.

9. Nichols, D.E. and Glennon, R.A. Medicinal chemistry and structure-activity relationships of hallucinogens. In B.L. Jacobs (Ed.), *Hallucinogens: Neurochemical, Behavioral, and Clinical Perspectives*. New York: Raven Press, 1984.

10. Shulgin, A.T. and Nichols, D.E. Characterization of three new psychotomimetics. In R.C. Stillman and R.E. Willette (Eds.), *The Psychopharmacology of Hallucinogens*. Elmsford, NY: Pergamon Press, 1978, p. 77.

11. Nichols, D.E. and Oberlender, R. Structure-activity relationships of MDMA-like substances. In K. Asghar and E. De Souza (Eds.), *Pharmacology and Toxicology of Amphetamine and Related Designer Drugs*. NIDA Research Monograph 94 (DHHS Publication No. [ADM]89-1640). Washington, DC: Department of Health and Human Services, 1989.

12. Nichols, D.E., Hoffman, A.J., Oberlender, R.A., Jacob, P., and Shulgin, A.T. Derivatives of 1-(1,3-benzodioxol-5-yl)-2-butanamine: Representatives of a novel therapeutic class. *Journal of Medicinal Chemistry*, 1986, 29:2009-2015.

13. Braun, U., Shulgin, A.T., and Braun, G. Centrally active N-substituted analogs of 3,4-methylenedioxyphenylisopropylamine (3,4-methylenedioxyamphetamine). *Journal of Pharmaceutical Sciences,* 1980, 69:192-195.

14. Buchanan, J. Ecstasy in the emergency department. *Clinical Toxicology Update*, 1985, 7:1-4.

15. Anderson, G.M., Braun, G., Braun, U., Nichols, D.E., and Shulgin, A.T. Absolute configuration and psychomimetic activity. In G. Barnett, M. Trsic, and R. Willette (Eds.), *QuaSAR Research Monograph 22.* Washington, DC: National Institute on Drug Abuse, 1978.

16. Shulgin, A.T. (personal communication, January 1995).

17. Hayner, G.N. and McKinney, H. MDMA: The dark side of Ecstasy. *Journal of Psychoactive Drugs,* 1986, 18:341-347.

18. Metzner, R. The great entactogen-empathogen debate. *MAPS Newsletter,* 1993, IV(2):48-49.

19. Nichols, D.E. Differences between the mechanism of action of MDMA, MBDB, and the classic hallucinogens: Identification of a new therapeutic class: Entactogens. *Journal of Psychoactive Drugs,* 1986, 18:305-313.

20. Nichols, D.E. (personal communication, November 1995).

21. Nichols, D.E. The great entactogen-empathogen debate. *MAPS Newsletter,* 1993, IV(2):47.

22. Callaway, C.W., Rempel, N., Peng, R.Y., and Geyer, M.A. Serotonin $5HT_1$-like receptors mediate hyperactivity in rats induced by 3,4-methylenedioxymethamphetamine. *Neuropsychopharmacology,* 1992, 7:113-127.

23. Nichols, D.E., Lloyd, D.H., Hoffman, A.J., Nichols, M.B., and Yim, G.K.W. Effects of certain hallucinogenic amphetamine analogues on the release of [^{3}H]serotonin from rat brain synaptosomes. *Journal of Medicinal Chemistry,* 1982, 25:530-535.

24. Rattray, M. Ecstasy: Towards an understanding of the biochemical basis of the actions of MDMA. *Essays in Biochemistry,* 1991, 26:77-87.

25. Battaglia, G., Zaczek, R., and De Souza, E.B. MDMA effects in brain: Pharmacologic profile and evidence of neurotoxicity from neurochemical and autoradiographic studies. In S. J. Peroutka (Ed.), *Ecstasy: The Clinical, Pharmacological, and Neurotoxicological Effects of the Drug MDMA.* Boston, MA: Kluwer Academic Publishers, 1990.

26. Pan, H.S. and Wang, R.Y. The action of (+/-)-MDMA on medial prefrontal cortical neurons is mediated through the serotonergic system. *Brain Research,* 1991, 543:56-60.

27. Nash, J.F. and Brodkin, J. Microdialysis studies on 3,4-methylenedioxymethamphetamine-induced dopamine release: Effect of dopamine uptake inhibitors. *Journal of Pharmacology and Experimental Therapeutics,* 1991, 259:820-825.

28. McCann, U.D. and Ricaurte, G.A. Use and abuse of ring-substituted amphetamines. In A. Cho and D.S. Segal (Eds.), *Amphetamine and its Analogs.* New York: Academic Press, 1994.

29. Bilsky, E.J., Hui, Y., Hubbell, C.L., and Reid, L.D. Methylenedioxy-methamphetamine capacity to establish place preferences and modify intake of an alcohol beverage. *Pharmacology, Biochemistry, and Behavior,* 1990, 37:633-638.

30. Schechter, M.D. Serotonergic-dopaminergic mediation of 3,4-methylenedioxymethamphetamine (MDMA, "Ecstasy"). *Pharmacology, Biochemistry, and Behavior,* 1989, 31:817-824.

31. Schmidt, C.J. and Kehne, J.H. Neurotoxicity of MDMA: Neurochemical effects. *Annals of the New York Academy of Science*, 1990, 600:665-681.

32. Schmidt, C.J. Neurotoxicity of the psychedelic amphetamine, methylenedioxymethamphetamine. *Journal of Pharmacology and Experimental Therapeutics*, 1987, 240:1-7.

33. Insel, T.R., Battaglia, G.A., Johannessen, J.N., Marra, S., and De Souza, E.B. 3,4-Methylenedioxymethamphetamine ("Ecstasy") selectively destroys brain serotonin terminals in rhesus monkeys. *Journal of Pharmacology and Experimental Therapeutics*, 1989, 249:713-720.

34. Steele, T.D., McCann, U.D., and Ricaurte, G.A. 3,4-Methylenedioxymethamphetamine (MDMA, "Ecstasy"): Pharmacology and toxicology in animals and humans. *Addiction*, 1994, 89:539-551.

35. Stone, D.M., Stahl, D.C., Hanson, G.R., and Gibb, J.W. The effects of 3,4-methylenedioxymethamphetamine (MDMA) and 3,4-methylenedioxyamphetamine (MDA) on monoaminergic systems in the rat brain. *European Journal of Pharmacology*, 1986, 128:41-48.

36. Schmidt, C.J., Wu, L., and Lovenberg, W. Methylenedioxymethamphetamine: A potentially neurotoxic amphetamine analogue. *European Journal of Pharmacology*, 1986, 124:175-178.

37. Slikker, W., Ali, S.F., Scallet, A.C., Firth, C.H., Newport, G.D., and Bailey, J.R. Neurochemical and neurohistological alterations in the rat and monkey produced by orally administered methylenedioxymethamphetamine (MDMA). *Toxicology and Applied Pharmacology*, 1988, 94:448-457.

38. Ricaurte, G.A., DeLanney, L.E., Wiener, S.G., Irwin, I., and Langston, J.W. 5-Hydroxyindoleacetic acid in cerebrospinal fluid reflects serotonergic damage induced by 3,4-methylenedioxymethamphetamine in CNS of non-human primates. *Brain Research*, 1988, 474:359-363.

39. Frith, C.H., Chang, L.W., Lattin, D.L., Walls, R.C., Hamm, J., and Doblin, R. Toxicity of methylenedioxymethamphetamine (MDMA) in the dog and the rat. *Fundamental and Applied Toxicology*, 1987, 9:110-119.

40. Commins, D.L., Vosmer, G., Virus, R.M., Woolverton, C.R., Schuster, C.R., and Seiden, L.S. Biochemical and histological evidence that methylenedioxymethamphetamine (MDMA) is toxic to neurons in rat brain. *Journal of Pharmacology and Experimental Therapeutics*, 1987, 241:338-345.

41. Grob, C.S. and Poland, R.E. MDMA. In J.H. Lowinson, P. Ruiz, R.B. Millman, and J.G. Langrod (Eds.), *Substance Abuse: A Comprehensive Textbook.* Baltimore, MD: Williams & Wilkins, 1997.

42. Ricaurte, G.A., Finnegan, K.T., Irwin, I., and Langston, J.W. Aminergic metabolites in cerebrospinal fluid of humans previously exposed to MDMA: Preliminary observations. *Annals of the New York Academy of Sciences*, 1990, 600:699-710.

43. Peroutka, S.J., Pascoe, N., and Faull, K.F. Monoamine metabolites in the cerebrospinal fluid of recreational users of 3,4-methylenedioxymethamphetamine (MDMA, "Ecstasy"). *Research Communications in Substance Abuse*, 1987, 8:125-138.

44. Bryden, A.A., Rothwell, P.J.N., and O'Reilly, P.H. Urinary retention with misuse of "Ecstasy." *British Medical Journal,* 1995, 310:504.

45. Polkis, A., Fitzgerald, R.L., Hall, K.V., and Saady, J.J. Emit-d.a.u. monoclonal amphetamine/methamphetamine assay. II. Detection of methylenedioxy-amphetamine (MDA) and methylenedioxymethamphetamine (MDMA). *Forensic Science International,* 1993, 59:63-70.

46. Hughes, J.C., McCabe, M., and Evans, R.J. Intracranial haemorrhage with ingestion of "Ecstasy." *Archives of Emergency Medicine,* 1993, 10:372-374.

47. McCann, U.D. and Ricaurte, G.A. Lasting neuropsychiatric sequelae of methylenedioxymethamphetamine ("Ecstasy") in recreational users. *Journal of Clinical Psychopharmacology,* 1991, 11:302-305.

48. McCann, U.D. and Ricaurte, G.A. Reinforcing subjective effects of (+/-) 3,4-methylenedioxymethamphetamine ("Ecstasy") may be separable from its neurotoxic actions: Clinical evidence. *Journal of Clinical Psychopharmacology,* 1993, 13:214-217.

49. Hansson, R.C. Clandestine laboratories: Production of MDMA (3,4-methylenedioxymethamphetamine). *Analog,* 1987, 9:1-10.

50. Shulgin, A.T. The background and chemistry of MDMA. *Journal of Psychoactive Drugs,* 1986, 18:291-304.

51. Shulgin, A.T. History of MDMA. In S.J. Peroutka (Ed.), *Ecstasy: The Clinical, Pharmacological, and Neurotoxicological Effects of the Drug MDMA.* Boston, MA: Kluwer Academic Publishers, 1990.

52. Doblin, R. and Goldsmith, N.M. "Ecstasy" drug tests employ high doses. *The New York Times,* August 24, 1995, Sec. Op/ed, p. 24.

53. Cohen, R.S. and Cocores, J. Neuropsychiatric manifestations following the use of 3,4-methylenedioxymethamphetamine (MDMA; "Ecstasy"). *Progress in Neuro-Psychopharmacology and Biological Psychiatry,* 1997, 21:727-734.

Chapter 3

1. Shulgin, A.T. History of MDMA. In S.J. Peroutka (Ed.), *Ecstasy: The Clinical, Pharmacological and Neurotoxicological Effects of the Drug MDMA.* Boston, MA: Kluwer Academic Publishers, 1990.

2. Beck, J. The public health implications of MDMA use. In S.J. Peroutka (Ed.), *Ecstasy: The Clinical, Pharmacological and Neurotoxicological Effects of the Drug MDMA.* Boston, MA: Kluwer Academic Publishers, 1990.

3. Peroutka, S.J. Recreational use of MDMA. In S.J. Peroutka (Ed.), *Ecstasy: The Clinical, Pharmacological and Neurotoxicological Effects of the Drug MDMA.* Boston, MA: Kluwer Academic Publishers, 1990.

4. Mullen, F.M. Schedules of controlled substances; Proposed placement of 3,4-methylenedioxymethamphetamine (MDMA) into Schedule I. *Federal Register,* 1984, 49:30,210.

5. Mullen, F.M. Schedules of controlled substances; Proposed placement of 3,4-methylenedioxymethamphetamine (MDMA) into Schedule I. *Federal Register,* 1984, 49:50,732-50,733.

6. McClain, H. (personal communication, November 1995).

7. Young, F.L. MDMA Administrative Law Hearings, United States Department of Justice, Drug Enforcement Administration, Prehearing conference, 1985, Docket No. 84-48.

8. Lawn, J.C. Schedules of controlled substances; Temporary placement of 3,4-methylenedioxymethamphetamine (MDMA) into Schedule I. *Federal Register*, 1985, 50:23,118-23,120.

9. Ricaurte, G.A, Bryan, G., Strauss, L., Seiden, L., and Schuster, L. Hallucinogenic amphetamine selectively destroys brain serotonin nerve terminals. *Science*, 1985, 229:986-988.

10. Grinspoon, L. Testimony on behalf of Drs. Grinspoon and Greer, Professors Bakalar and Roberts, United States Department of Justice, MDMA Administrative Law Hearings, 1985, Docket No. 84-48.

11. Roberts, T.B. Testimony on behalf of Drs. Grinspoon and Greer, Professors Bakalar and Roberts, United States Department of Justice, MDMA Administrative Law Hearings, 1985, Docket No. 84-48.

12. Greer, G. MDMA: A new psychotropic compound and its effects in humans. Privately published, 1983.

13. Greer, G. Testimony on behalf of Drs. Grinspoon and Greer, Professors Bakalar and Roberts, United States Department of Justice, MDMA Administrative Law Hearings, 1985, Docket No. 84-48.

14. Greer, G. and Tolbert, R. Subjective reports of the effects of MDMA in a clinical setting. *Journal of Psychoactive Drugs*, 1986, 18:319-327.

15. Shulgin, A.T. Personal letter to George Greer. Testimony submitted in the MDMA Administrative Law Hearings, 1985, Docket 84-48.

16. Lynch, R. Testimony on behalf of Drs. Grinspoon and Greer, Professors Bakalar and Roberts, United States Department of Justice, MDMA Administrative Law Hearings, 1985, Docket No. 84-48.

17. Wolfson, P.E. Testimony on behalf of Drs. Grinspoon and Greer, Professors Bakalar and Roberts, United States Department of Justice, MDMA Administrative Law Hearings, 1985, Docket No. 84-48.

18. Strassman, R.J. Testimony on behalf of Drs. Grinspoon and Greer, Professors Bakalar and Roberts, United States Department of Justice, MDMA Administrative Law Hearings, 1985, Docket No. 84-48, p. 3.

19. Shulgin, A.T. (personal communication, January 1995).

20. Shannon, H.E. Testimony on behalf of the Drug Enforcement Administration, United States Department of Justice, MDMA Administrative Law Hearings, 1985, Docket No. 84-48.

21. Kleinman, J.E. Testimony on behalf of the Drug Enforcement Administration, United States Department of Justice, MDMA Administrative Law Hearings, 1985, Docket No. 84-48.

22. Seiden, L.S. Testimony on behalf of the Drug Enforcement Administration, United States Department of Justice, MDMA Administrative Law Hearings, 1985, Docket No. 84-48, pp. 1-2.

23. Siegel, R.K. Testimony on behalf of the Drug Enforcement Administration, United States Department of Justice, MDMA Administrative Law Hearings, 1985, Docket No. 84-48, p. 4.

24. Klein, J. The new drug they call Ecstasy: Is it too much to swallow? *New York Magazine*, 1985, 18:38-43.

25. Docherty, J.P. Testimony on behalf of the Drug Enforcement Administration, United States Department of Justice, MDMA Administrative Law Hearings, 1985, Docket No. 84-48.

26. Tocus, E.C. Testimony on behalf of the Drug Enforcement Administration, United States Department of Justice, MDMA Administrative Law Hearings, 1985, Docket No. 84-48.

27. Young, F.L. Opinion and recommended ruling, findings of fact, conclusions of law and decision of Administrative Law Judge, United States Department of Justice, Drug Enforcement Administration, MDMA Administrative Law Hearings, 1986, Docket No. 84-48.

28. Beck, J. and Rosenbaum, M. *Pursuit of Ecstasy: The MDMA Experience.* Albany, NY: SUNY Press, 1994.

29. Lawn, J.C. Schedules of controlled substances; Extension of temporary control of 3,4-methylenedioxymethamphetamine (MDMA) in Schedule I. *Federal Register*, 1986, 51:21,911-21,912.

30. Joranson, D.E. Exceptions to the opinion and ruling, United States Department of Justice, Drug Enforcement Administration, MDMA Administrative Law Hearings, 1986, Docket No. 84-48.

31. Lawn, J.C. Schedules of controlled substances; Scheduling of 3,4-methylenedioxymethamphetamine (MDMA) into Schedule I of the Controlled Substances Act. *Federal Register*, 1986, 51:36,552-36,560.

32. Lawn, J.C. Schedules of controlled substances; Deletion of 3,4-methylenedioxymethamphetamine (MDMA) from Schedule I of the Controlled Substances Act. *Federal Register*, 1988, 53:2,225.

33. Lawn, J.C. Schedules of controlled substances; Scheduling of 3,4-methylenedioxymethamphetamine (MDMA) into Schedule I of the Controlled Substances Act; Remand. *Federal Register*, 1988, 53:5,156.

34. Downing, J. The psychological and physiological effects of MDMA on normal volunteers. *Journal of Psychoactive Drugs*, 1986, 18:335-340.

35. Adamson, S. *Through the Gateway of the Heart: Accounts of Experiences with MDMA and Other Empathogenic Substances.* San Francisco, CA: Four Trees Publications, 1985.

36. Goldstein, R. The facts about "Ecstasy": A talk with Andrew Weil. *Voice*, February 7, 1989:31.

Chapter 4

1. Malitz, S. The role of mescaline and d-lysergic acid in psychiatric treatment. *Diseases of the Nervous System*, 1966, 7:39-42.

2. Joralemon, D. The role of hallucinogenic drugs and sensory stimuli in Pervian ritual healing. *Culture, Medicine, and Psychiatry*, 1984, 8:399.

3. Denber, H.C.B. Mescaline and lysergic acid diethylamide: Therapeutic implications of the drug-induced state. *Diseases of the Nervous System*, 1969, 30:24.

4. Shulgin, A.T. and Nichols, D.E. Characterization of three new psychotomimetics. In R.C. Stillman and R.E. Willette (Eds.), *The Psychopharmacology of Hallucinogens*. Elmsford, NY: Pergamon Press, 1978.

5. Grinspoon, L. and Bakalar, J.B. Can drugs be used to enhance the psychotherapeutic process. *American Journal of Psychotherapy*, 1986, XL:393-404.

6. Adamson, S. *Through the Gateway of the Heart: Accounts of Experiences with MDMA and Other Empathogenic Substances*. San Francisco, CA: Four Trees Publications, 1985.

7. Seymour, R. *MDMA*. San Francisco, CA: Haight Ashbury Publications, 1986.

8. Adamson, S. and Metzner, R. The nature of the MDMA experience and its role in healing, psychotherapy, and spiritual practice. *Revision*, 1988, 10:59-72.

9. Downing, J. Testimony on behalf of Drs. Grinspoon and Greer, Professors Bakalar and Roberts, United States Department of Justice, MDMA Administrative Law Hearings, 1985, Docket No. 84-48.

10. Rosenbaum, M. and Doblin, R. Why MDMA should not have been made illegal. In J.A. Inciardi (Ed.), *The Drug Legalization Debate*. Newbury Park, CA: Sage Publications, 1991, p. 136.

11. Corwin, M. Psychiatrists defend new street drug for therapy. *Los Angeles Times*, May 27, 1985, Sec. A:1, A:16.

12. Wolfson, P.E. Testimony on behalf of Drs. Grinspoon and Greer, Professors Bakalar and Roberts, United States Department of Justice, MDMA Administrative Law Hearings, 1985, Docket No. 84-48.

13. Greer, G. Using MDMA in psychotherapy. *Advances*, 1985, 2:57-59.

14. Greer, G. and Tolbert, R. Subjective reports of the effects of MDMA in a clinical setting. *Journal of Psychoactive Drugs*, 1986, 18:319-327.

15. Greer, G. MDMA: A new psychotropic compound and its effects in humans. Privately published, 1983.

16. Roberts, T.B. Testimony on behalf of Drs. Grinspoon and Greer, Professors Bakalar and Roberts, United States Department of Justice, MDMA Administrative Law Hearings, 1985, Docket No. 84-48.

17. Shulgin, A.T. Twenty years on an ever-changing quest. In L. Grinspoon and J.B. Bakalar (Eds.), *Psychedelic Reflections*. New York: Human Science Press, 1983.

18. Downing, J. The psychological and physiological effects of MDMA on normal volunteers. *Journal of Psychoactive Drugs*, 1986, 18:335-340.

19. Yensen, R. Testimony on behalf of Drs. Grinspoon and Greer, Professors Bakalar and Roberts, United States Department of Justice, MDMA Administrative Law Hearings, 1985, Docket No. 84-48.

20. Ingrasci, R. Testimony on behalf of Drs. Grinspoon and Greer, Professors Bakalar and Roberts, United States Department of Justice, MDMA Administrative Law Hearings, 1985, Docket No. 84-48.

21. Eisner, B. (Preface). *Ecstasy: The MDMA Story.* Berkeley, CA: Ronin, 1989, p. 64.

22. Beck, J. and Rosenbaum, M. *Pursuit of Ecstasy: The MDMA Experience.* Albany, NY: SUNY Press, 1994.

23. Grob, C.S., Poland, R.E., Chang, L., and Ernst, T. Psychobiological effects of 3,4-methylenedioxymethamphetamine in humans: Methodological considerations and preliminary observations. *Behavioural Brain Research*, 1996, 73:103-107.

24. Siegel, S. Drug dissociation in the nineteenth century. In F.C. Colpaert and J.L. Slangen (Eds.), *Drug Discrimination: Applications in CNS Pharmacology.* Amsterdam, Netherlands: Elsevier Biomedical Press, 1982.

Chapter 5

1. Weil, A. and Rosen, W. *From Chocolate to Morphine.* Boston, MA: Houghton Mifflin, 1993.

2. O'Hagan, S. Raving madness. *The Times*, February 22, 1992, Sec. 10A-12A.

3. Klein, J. The new drug they call Ecstasy: Is it too much to swallow? *New York Magazine,* 1985, 18:38-43.

4. McKusick, T. Catch a rave: Is this new drug-and-dance scene a triumph of tribalism—or the disco of the '90s? *Utne Reader,* 1992, September/October: 23-24.

5. McDowell, D. (personal communication, November 1994).

6. Rader, R. Dark side of pop craze surfaces: "Ecstasy" blamed in woman's death. *Houston Post,* November 13, 1988, Sec. A26.

7. Cohen, R.S. Subjective reports on the effects of the MDMA ("Ecstasy") experience in humans. *Progress in Neuro-Psychopharmacology and Biological Psychiatry,* 1995, 19:1137-1145.

8. Peroutka, S.J., Newman, H., and Harris, H. Subjective effects of 3,4-methylenedioxymethamphetamine in recreational users. *Neuropsychopharmacology,* 1988, 1:273-277.

9. McDowell, D. Ecstasy and raves: The '90s party scene. In M.W. Fischman (Chair), *Hallucinogens, LSD, and Raves.* Symposium conducted at the National Press Club, Washington, DC, 1993.

10. Tyler, A. *Street Drugs.* London, England: Hodder and Stoughton, 1995.

11. Bumiller, E. U.S. claims 2 nightclubs are drug bazaars. *The New York Times,* May 16, 1996, Sec. B1, B8.

12. LSD on a comeback in London: Private drug use gives way to '60s-style group encounters. *Chicago Tribune,* August 18, 1988, Sec. A27.

13. Peroutka, S.J. Incidence of recreational use of 3,4-methylenedioxyme-thamphetamine (MDMA; "Ecstasy") on an undergraduate campus. *New England Journal of Medicine,* 1987, 317:1542-1543.

14. Keller, W.F. Ecstasy: The high school "chic" drug. *Parenting Today,* 1988, 1:2.

15. Cuomo, M.J., Dyment, P.G., and Gammino, V.M. Increasing use of "Ecstasy" (MDMA) and other hallucinogens on a college campus. *Journal of American College Health,* 1994, 42:271-274.

16. Randall, T. "Rave" scene, Ecstasy use, leap Atlantic. *Journal of the American Medical Association,* 1992, 268:1506.

17. Miller, N.S. and Gold, M.S. LSD and Ecstasy: Pharmacology, phenomenology, and treatment. *Psychiatric Annals,* 1994, 24:131-133.

18. Millman, R.B. and Beeder, A.B. The new psychedelic culture: LSD, Ecstasy, "rave" parties, and the Grateful Dead. *Psychiatric Annals,* 1994, 24:148-150.

19. Solowij, N., Hall, W., and Lee, N. Recreational MDMA use in Sydney: A profile of "Ecstasy" users and their experiences with the drug. *British Journal of Addictions,* 1992, 87:1161-1172.

20. Liester, M.B., Grob, C.S., Bravo, G.L., and Walsh, R.N. Phenomenology and sequelae of 3,4-methylenedioxymethamphetamine use. *Journal of Nervous and Mental Disease,* 1992, 180:345-352.

21. Cregg, M.T. and Tracey, J.A. Ecstasy abuse in Ireland. *Irish Medical Journal,* 1993, 86:118-120.

Chapter 6

1. Miller, M.S. Bad trips: How they happen. In S.H. Snyder (Ed.), *The Encyclopedia of Psychoactive Drugs.* New York: Chelsea House, 1988.

2. Tyler, A. *Street Drugs.* London, England: Hodder and Stoughton, 1995.

3. McDowell, D.M. and Kleber, H.D. MDMA: Its history and pharmacology. *Psychiatric Annals,* 1994, 24:127-130.

4. Cohen, R.S. Subjective reports on the effects of the MDMA ("Ecstasy") experience in humans. *Progress in Neuro-Psychopharmacology and Biological Psychiatry,* 1995, 19:1137-1145.

5. McCoy, E.P, Renfrew, C., Johnston, J.R., and Lavery, G. Malignant hyperpyrexia in an MDMA ("Ecstasy") abuser. *The Ulster Medical Journal,* 1994, 63:103-107.

6. Hayner, G.N. and McKinney, H. MDMA: The dark side of ecstasy. *Journal of Psychoactive Drugs,* 1986, 18:341-347.

7. Series, H. and Lindefors, N. Ecstasy-Verkningar och toxicitet. *Lakartidningen,* 1993, 90:2648-2652.

8. McCann, U.D. and Ricaurte, G.A. MDMA ("Ecstasy") and panic disorder: Induction by a single dose. *Biological Psychiatry,* 1992, 32:950-953.

9. Pallanti, S. and Mazzi, D. MDMA ("Ecstasy") precipitation of panic disorder. *Biological Psychiatry,* 1992, 32:91-95.

10. Whitaker-Azmitia, P.M. and Aronson, T.A. "Ecstasy" (MDMA)-induced panic. *American Journal of Psychiatry,* 1989, 146:119.

11. Schifano, F. and Magni, G. MDMA ("Ecstasy") abuse: Psychopathological features and craving for chocolate: A case series. *Biological Psychiatry,* 1994, 36:763-767.

12. McGuire, P. and Fahy, T. Chronic paranoid psychosis after misuse of MDMA ("Ecstasy"). *British Medical Journal,* 1991, 302:697.

13. Series, H., Boeles, S., Dorkins, E., and Peveler, R. Psychiatric complications of "Ecstasy" use. *Journal of Psychopharmacology,* 1994, 8:60-61.

14. Schifano, F. Chronic atypical psychosis associated with MDMA ("Ecstasy") abuse. *Lancet,* 1991, 338:1335.

15. Roberts, L. and Wright, H. Survival following intentional massive overdose of "Ecstasy." *Journal of Accident and Emergency Medicine,* 1993, 11:53-54.

16. Wodarz, N. and Boning, J. "Ecstasy"-induziertes psychotisches depersonalisationssyndrom. *Nevenarzt,* 1993, 64:478-480.

17. Creighton, F.J., Black, D.L., and Hyde, C.E. "Ecstasy" psychosis and flashbacks. *British Journal of Psychiatry,* 1991, 159:713-715.

18. Teggin, A.F. Ecstasy—a dangerous drug. *South African Medical Journal,* 1992, 81:431-432.

19. Benazzi, F. and Mazzoli, M. Psychiatric illness associated with "Ecstasy." *Lancet,* 1991, 338:1520.

20. Cox, D.E. "Rave" to the grave. *Forensic Science International,* 1993, 60:5-6.

21. Rohrig, T.P. and Prouty, R.W. Tissue distribution of methylenedioxymethamphetamine. *Journal of Analytical Toxicology,* 1992, 16:52-53.

22. Dowling, G.P. Human deaths and toxic reactions attributed to MDMA and MDEA. In S.J. Peroutka (Ed.), *Ecstasy: The Clinical, Pharmacological, and Neurotoxicological Effects of the Drug MDMA.* Boston, MA: Kluwer Academic Publishers, 1990.

23. Ellis, P. and Schimmel, P. Ecstasy abuse. *New Zealand Medical Journal,* 1989, 102:358.

24. Cohen, R.S. Adverse symptomatology and suicide associated with the use of methylenedioxymethamphetamine (MDMA; "Ecstasy"). *Biological Psychiatry,* 1996, 39:819-820.

25. Chiles, J. Drugs and suicide. In S.H. Snyder (Ed.), *The Encyclopedia of Psychoactive Drugs.* New York: Chelsea House, 1986.

26. Keenan, E., Gervin, M., Dorman, A., and O'Connor, J.J. Psychosis and recreational use of MDMA. *Irish Journal of Psychological Medicine,* 1993, 10:162-163.

27. Williams, H., Meagher, D., and Galligan, P. MDMA ("Ecstasy"): A case of possible drug-induced psychosis. *Irish Journal of Medical Science,* 1993, 162:43-44.

28. Cassidy, G. and Ballard, C.G. Psychiatric sequelae of MDMA (Ecstasy) and related drugs. *Irish Journal of Psychological Medicine,* 1994, 11:132-133.

29. McCann, U.D. and Ricaurte, G.A. Lasting neuropsychiatric sequelae of methylenedioxymethamphetamine ("Ecstasy") in recreational users. *Journal of Clinical Psychopharmacology,* 1991, 11:302-305.

30. McCann, U.D. and Ricaurte, G.A. Reinforcing subjective effects of (±) 3,4-methylenedioxymethamphetamine ("Ecstasy") may be separable from its neurotoxic actions: Clinical evidence. *Journal of Clinical Psychopharmacology,* 1993, 13:214-217.

31. Henry, J.A. Ecstasy and the dance of death. *British Medical Journal*, 1992, 305:5-6.

32. Oranje, W.A., von Pol, P., Wurf, A., Zeijen, R.N., Stockbrugger, R.W., and Arends, J.W. XTC-induced hepatitis. *Netherlands Journal of Medicine*, 1994, 44:56-59.

33. Gorard, D.A., Davies, S.E., and Clark, M.L. Misuse of ecstasy. *British Medical Journal*, 1992, 305:309.

34. Shearman, J.D., Satsangi, J., Chapman, R.W.G., Ryley, N.G., and Weatherhead, S. Misuse of ecstasy. *British Medical Journal*, 1992, 305:309.

35. Ijzermans, J.N.M., Tilanus, H.W., de Man, R.A., and Metselaar, H.J. Ecstasy and liver transplantation. *Annales de Medecine Interne*, 1993, 144:568.

36. Ellis, A.J., Wendon, J.A., Portmann, B., and Williams, R. Acute liver damage and ecstasy ingestion. *Gut*, 1996, 38:454-458.

37. Dykhuizen, R.S., Brunt, P.W., Atkinson, P., Simpson, J.G., and Smith, C.C. Ecstasy induced hepatitis mimicking viral hepatitis. *Gut*, 1995, 36:939-941.

38. de Man, R.A., Wilson, J.H.P., and Tjen, H.S.L.M. Acuut leverfalen door methyleneendioxymetamfetamine. *Ned Tijdschr Geneeskd*, 1993, 137:727-729.

39. Marsh, J.C.W., Abboudi, Z.H., Gibson, F.M., Scopes, J., Daly, S., O'Shaunnessy, D.F.O., Baughan, A.S.J., and Gordon-Smith, E.C. Aplastic anaemia following exposure to 3,4-methylenedioxymethamphetamine ("Ecstasy"). *British Journal of Haematology*, 1994, 88:281-285.

40. Lehmann, E., Thom, C.H., and Croft, D.N. Delayed severe rhabdomyolysis after taking "Ecstasy." *Postgraduate Medical Journal*, 1995, 71:186-187.

41. Fahal, I.H., Sallomi, D.F., Yaqoob, M., and Bell, G.M. Acute renal failure after Ecstasy. *British Medical Journal*, 1992, 305:29.

42. Cadier, M.A. and Clarke, J.A. Ecstasy and whizz at a rave resulting in major burn plus complications. *Burns*, 1993, 19:239-240.

43. Singarajah, C. and Lavies, N.G. An overdose of Ecstasy. *Anaesthesia*, 1992, 47:686-687.

44. Padkin, A. Treating MDMA ("Ecstasy") toxicity. *Anaesthesia*, 1994, 49:259.

45. Kessel, B. Hyponatraemia after ingestion of ecstasy. *British Medical Journal*, 1994, 308:414.

46. Maxwell, D.L., Polkey, M.I., and Henry, J.A. Hyponatraemia and catatonic stupor after taking "Ecstasy." *British Medical Journal*, 1993, 307:1399.

47. Lee, J.W. Catatonic stupor after "Ecstasy." *British Medical Journal*, 1994, 308:717-718.

48. Taylor, M. Catatonia: A review of the behavioral neurological syndrome. *Neuropsychiatry, Neuropsychology, and Behavioral Neurology*, 1990, 3:48-72.

49. Matthai, S.M., Sills, J.A., Davidson, D.C., and Alexandrou, D. Cerebral Oedema after ingestion of MDMA and unrestricted intake of water. *British Medical Journal*, 1996, 312:1359.

50. Brown, E.R.S., Jarvie, D.R., and Simpson, D. Use of drugs at "raves." *Scottish Medical Journal*, 1995, 40:168-171.

51. Finch, E., Sell, L., and Arnold, D. Drug workers emphasize that water is not an antidote to drug. *British Medical Journal*, 1996, 313:690.

52. Ecstasy update. *Druglink,* 1996, 11:1.

53. Holden, R. and Jackson, M.A. Near-fatal hyponatraemic coma due to vaso-pressin oversecretion after "Ecstasy" (3,4-MDMA). *Lancet,* 1996, 347:1052.

54. Gledhill, J.A., Moore, D.F., Bell, D., and Henry, J.A. Subarachnoid hae-morrhage associated with MDMA abuse. *Journal of Neurology, Neurosurgery, and Psychiatry,* 1993, 56:1036-1037.

55. Hughes, J.C., McCabe, M., and Evans, R.J. Intracranial haemorrhage with ingestion of "Ecstasy." *Archives of Emergency Medicine,* 1993, 10:372-374.

56. Harries, D.P. and De Silva, R. "Ecstasy" and intracerebral haemorrhage. *Scottish Medical Journal,* 1992, 37:150-152.

57. Screaton, G.R., Singer, M., Cairns, H.S., Thrasher, A., Sarner, M., and Cohen, S.L. Hyperpyrexia and rhabdomyolysis after MDMA ("Ecstasy") abuse. *Lancet,* 1992, 339:677-678.

58. Manchanda, S. and Connolly, M.J. Cerebral infarction in association with Ecstasy abuse. *Postgraduate Medical Journal,* 1993, 69:874-875.

59. Hanyu, S., Kunihiko, I., Imai, H., Imai, N., and Yoshida, M. Cerebral infarc-tion associated with 3,4-methylenedioxymethamphetamine ("Ecstasy") abuse. *European Neurology,* 1995, 35:173.

60. Hardebo, J.E., Edvinsson, L., Owman, C.H., and Svendgaad, N.A. Potenti-ation and antagonism of serotonin effects on intracranial and extracranial vessels: Possible implications of migraine. *Neurology,* 1978, 28:64-70.

61. Cohen, R.S. and Cocores, J. Neuropsychiatric manifestations following the use of 3,4-methylenedioxymethamphetamine (MDMA; "Ecstasy"). *Progress in Neuro-Psychopharmacology and Biological Psychiatry,* 1997, 21:727-734.

62. Bryden, A.A., Rothwell, P.J.N., and O'Reilly, P.H. Urinary retention with misuse of "Ecstasy." *British Medical Journal,* 1995, 310:504.

63. Henriksen, T. Incontinence after stroke. *Lancet,* 1991, 338:1335.

64. Rothwell, P.M. and Grant, R. Cerebral venous sinus thrombosis induced by "Ecstasy." *Journal of Neurology, Neurosurgery, and Psychiatry,* 1993, 56:1035.

65. Levine, A.J., Drew, S., and Rees, G.M. "Ecstasy" induced pneumomedias-tinum. *Journal of the Royal Society of Medicine,* 1993, 86:232-233.

66. Suarez, R.V. and Riemersma, R. "Ecstasy" and sudden cardiac death. *The American Journal of Forensic Medicine and Pathology,* 1988, 9:339-341.

67. Logan, A., Stickle, B., O'Keefe, N., and Hewitson, H. Survival following "Ecstasy" ingestion with a peak temperature of 42°C. *Anaesthesia,* 1993, 48:1017-1018.

68. Milroy, C.M., Clark, J.C., and Forrest, A.R.W. Pathology of deaths associated with "Ecstasy" and "Eve" misuse. *Journal of Clinical Pathology,* 1996, 49:149-153.

69. Dowling, G.P., McDonough, E.T., and Bost, R.O. "Eve" and "Ecstasy": A report of five deaths associated with the use of MDEA and MDMA. *Journal of the American Medical Association,* 1987, 257:1615-1617.

70. Bost, R.O. 3,4-Methylenedioxymethamphetamine (MDMA) and other amphetamine derivatives. *Journal of Forensic Sciences,* 1988, 33:576-587.

71. Forrest, A.R.W., Galloway, J.H., Marsh, I.D., Strachan, G.A., and Clark, J.C. A fatal overdose with 3,4-methylenedioxyamphetamine derivatives. *Forensic Science International,* 1994, 64:57-59.

72. Henry, J.A., Jeffreys, K.J., and Dawling, S. Toxicity and deaths from 3,4-methylenedioxymethamphetamine ("Ecstasy"). *Lancet,* 1992, 340:384-387.

73. Campkin, N.T.A. and Davies, U.M. Another death from Ecstasy. *Journal of the Royal Society of Medicine,* 1992, 85:6.

74. Brown, C. and Osterloh, J. Multiple severe complications from recreational ingestion of MDMA ("Ecstasy"). *Journal of the American Medical Association,* 1987, 258:780-781.

75. Chadwick, I.S., Linsley, A., Freemont, A.J., Doran, B., and Curry, P.D. Ecstasy, 3,4-methylenedioxymethamphetamine (MDMA), a fatality associated with coagulopathy and hyperthermia. *Journal of the Royal Society of Medicine,* 1991, 84:371.

76. Platt, S. Moral panic. *New Statesman and Society.* November 24, 1995. 8:14-15.

77. Ecstasy and the agony. *The Times,* March 19, 1995, Sec. Family Life:22-23.

78. Jones, T. Teenager dies and friends critically ill after taking Ecstasy. *The Times,* September 30, 1995, Sec. Home News:7.

79. Teenage water ski champion died after Ecstasy trip. *The Times,* May 17, 1994, Sec. B:3.

80. Teenager dies after all-night rave party. *The Times,* May 2, 1994, Sec. G:2.

81. Elliott, C. Hunt for dealer after drug deaths. *The Times,* May 3, 1994, Sec. G:4.

82. Boy 15 dies after taking Ecstasy pill. *The Times,* February 22, 1994, Sec. G:5.

83. Strassman, R. Adverse reactions to psychedelic drugs: A review of the literature. *Journal of Nervous and Mental Disease,* 1984, 172:577-595.

84. Wolff, K., Hay, A.W.M., Sherlock, K., and Conner, M. Contents of "Ecstasy." *Lancet,* 1995, 346:1100-1101.

85. Zinberg, N. *Drugs, Set, and Setting.* New Haven: Yale University Press, 1984.

86. Kaskey, G.B. Possible interaction between an MAOI and "Ecstasy." *American Journal of Psychiatry,* 1992, 149:411-412.

87. Smilkstein, M.J., Smolinske, S.C., and Rumack, B.H. A case of MAO inhibitor/MDMA interaction: Agony after Ecstasy. *Clinical Toxicology,* 1987, 25:149-159.

88. Squier, M.V., Jalloh, S., Jones-Hilton, D., and Series, H. Death after Ecstasy ingestion: Neuropathological findings. *Journal of Neurology, Neurosurgery, and Psychiatry,* 1995, 58:756-764.

Chapter 7

1. Craig, O. E is for agony. *The Times,* May 12, 1996, Sec. A:14.

2. Platt, S. Moral panic. *New Statesman and Society,* November 24, 1995, 8:14-15.

3. Ecstasy girl says: Never again. *The Times,* January 13, 1996, Sec. C:1.

4. Horsnell, M. Parents tell inquest of frantic fight to save Leah. *The Times,* February 1, 1996, Sec. A:3.

5. Walking on the moon. *Lancet,* 1996, 347:207.

6. Beck, J. and Rosenbaum, M. *Pursuit of Ecstasy: The MDMA Experience.* Albany, NY: SUNY Press, 1994.

Chapter 8

1. Platt, S. Moral panic. *New Statesman and Society,* November 24, 1995, 8:14-15.

2. Wallack, L. and Corbett, K. Illicit drug, tobacco, and alcohol use among youth: Trends and promising approaches in prevention. In H. Resnick (Ed.), *Youth and Drugs: Society's Mixed Messages.* OSAP Prevention Monograph, (DHHS Publication No. [ADM]90-1689). Rockville, MD: U.S. Department of Health and Human Services, 1990.

Glossary

acid: the most popular nickname used for LSD.

acute: intense symptoms with a rapid onset, typically brief in duration.

analgesic: a drug that relieves pain.

anemia: reduction in the quantity of the oxygen-carrying pigment hemoglobin in the blood.

anorectic: an agent taken to curb one's appetite.

antidiuretic: a drug that reduces urine flow.

ataxia: loss of coordinated movement caused typically by a disturbance in the nervous system.

autopsy: examination of a dead body to determine the cause of death.

bad trip: an unpleasant drug experience characterized by adverse or disturbing symptoms.

bruxism: involuntary clenching or grinding of the teeth.

candy flipping: ingesting both LSD and Ecstasy at or about the same time.

catatonia: a state of rigidity of the muscles, producing immobility.

clandestine: existing or done in secrecy (e.g., clandestine drug manufacture).

CNS: central nervous system.

coagulation: formation of a blood clot.

coma: complete loss of consciousness.

computed tomography (CT): diagnostic tool used to examine soft tissues of the body.

conviviality: sociability; talkativeness.

convulsions: temporary loss of consciousness with severe muscle contractions.

CSA: Controlled Substance Act.

CT: computed tomography.

DEA: Drug Enforcement Administration.

dehydration: loss or deficiency of water in the body tissues, resulting from improper water intake and rapid perspiration.

déjà vu: a vivid psychic experience in which immediate contemporary events seem to be a repetition of previous happenings. This is a common occurrence with those who have temporal lobe epilepsy.

depersonalization: a sensation of feeling outside or detached from one's body.

derealization: feeling as though one is in a dreamlike state. Surroundings seem unreal, foggy, or detached.

designer drug: a synthetic compound manufactured to mimic the effects of illicit narcotics, hallucinogens, stimulants, and depressants.

diaphoresis: perspiration.

DIC: disseminated intravascular coagulation.

disseminated intravascular coagulation (DIC): a disorder resulting from the overstimulation of the blood-clotting mechanisms.

Ecstasy: the most infamous nickname used for MDMA.

edema: excessive accumulation of fluid in the body tissues resulting in the swelling of a particular body area.

EEG: electroencephalogram.

efficacy: the power to bring about a desired result; overall effectiveness.

electroencephalogram (EEG): an instrument used to record the electrical activity from different brain regions.

encephalitis: inflammation of the brain.

epilepsy: abnormal brain wave activity; irregular discharges or firing of a cell. Depending upon the location of these discharges, symptoms can range from psychological manifestations and behavioral complications to actual convulsions.

euphoria: a feeling of well-being, elation, and exhilaration.

euthanasia: the deliberate, painless killing of persons who suffer from a painful or incurable disease or condition.

flashback: the spontaneous reoccurrence of a drug experience.

hallucinations: false perceptions about reality. Hallucinations may include hearing noises or seeing objects that are not really present.

hemorrhage: internal or external bleeding as a result of a ruptured blood vessel.

hepatitis: inflammation of the liver caused by viruses, toxic substances, or immunological abnormalities.

hyperpyrexia: abnormally high fever.

hypersomnia: sleep lasting excessively long periods of time.

hypertension: high blood pressure.

hyperthermia: exceptionally high body temperature.

hypertonicity: exceptionally high tension in muscles.

hyperventilation: breathing at an abnormally rapid rate while at rest.

hypoglycemia: a condition in which the level of blood sugar is abnormally low.

hyponatremia: abnormally low levels of sodium in the blood, typically occurring during dehydration.

impending doom: feeling that something bad is on the verge of occurring.

incontinence: inability to control the evacuation of the bladder.

insight: an understanding of oneself or one's situation.

insomnia: inability to sleep.

intoxication: the symptoms of poisoning due to ingestion of any toxic material.

jaundice: increase in bile pigment (bilirubin) in the blood causing yellow tinge to skin and eyes.

lethal dose (LD): the dose of a drug that produces a lethal effect in some percentage of the animals on which it is tested. An LD_{50} is the dose that would kill 50 percent of the animals to which a substance was administered.

lethargy: mental and physical sluggishness.

leukocytosis: increase in the number of white blood cells.

LSD: lysergic acid diethylamide.

MDA: 3,4-methylenedioxyamphetamine.

MDMA: 3,4-methylenedioxymethamphetamine, Ecstasy.

mydriasis: abnormal pupil dilation.

neurotransmitter: a chemical substance released from nerve endings to transmit impulses across synapses to other nerves.

nystagmus: jerking movement of the eyes.

organic: relating to any or all of the organs of the body.

paranoia: chronic psychosis characterized by fears, suspicion, and imaginary thoughts.

PCP: phencyclidine or angel dust.

pharmacological: pertains to the effects that drugs have on the body.

photosensitivity: to be affected by light or radiant energy.

placebo: an inactive drug, often used in experiments to make comparisons between experimental and control groups.

postmortem: see autopsy.

prophylactic: an agent that prevents the development of a condition or disease.

psychoactive drug: a chemical that changes mood, behavior, or thought processes. These agents exert their primary effects on the CNS.

psychopharmacological: pertains to the effects that drugs have on mental processes and behavior.

psychosis: severe mental illness in which one loses contact with reality.

psychotropic drug: a drug that affects psychic function, behavior, or experience.

pupil dilation: when the circular opening in the center of the iris opens widely. Pupillary dilation occurs due to stimulation of the sympathetic nervous system.

rapport: sympathetic or empathetic connection.

raves: all-night and into-the-morning dance parties typically held in open fields, empty warehouses, or city clubs. People gather together at a preplanned destination to dance and/or consume Ecstasy and/or LSD.

recreational drug: a substance that is taken for pleasure, most often at a social gathering.

renal failure: severe disturbance in the functioning of the kidneys.

repressed memories: memories that are unconsciously blocked from our conscious awareness. These include memories that may be too painful to deal with (e.g., childhood sexual trauma).

rhabdomyolysis: an acute, somtimes fatal disease marked by destruction of skeletal muscle. This may lead to renal failure.

seizures: see epilepsy.

sepsis: destruction of tissues by disease-causing bacteria or their toxins.

serotonin: 5-hydroxytryptamine (5-HT); a compound widely distributed in the tissues, particularly in the blood platelets, intestinal wall, and CNS. Serotonin also acts as a neurotransmitter. Abnormal serotonin function has been implicated in disturbances of sleep, appetite, mood, and psychiatric disorders, including depression and anxiety.

set: an expectation; a factor that determines people's reactions to drugs.

setting: the environment (e.g., physical, social); a factor that determines people's reactions to drugs.

stroke: occurs as a consequence of an interruption in the flow of blood to the brain. The result may vary in severity from a weakness or tingling in a limb to a profound paralysis, coma, or death.

suicidal ideations: the desire to deliberately hurt or try to kill oneself.

sympathomimetic: any drug that stimulates the sympathetic nervous system.

tachycardia: an abnormally rapid heart rate.

toxic: harmful, destructive, or deadly.

trip: a drug experience.

trismus: spasms in the jaw muscles.

vasoconstriction: a decrease in the diameter of blood vessels, mainly arteries.

vertigo: spinning sensation most often characterized by dizziness.

visceral sensations: sensations experienced within the body cavities, especially the organs of the abdominal cavities (e.g., stomach, intestines).

xerostomia: dryness of the mouth.

Bibliography

Abbott, A. and Concar, D. A trip into the unknown. *New Scientist*, 1992, 8:30-34.

Adamson, S. *Through the Gateway of the Heart: Accounts of Experiences with MDMA and Other Empathogenic Substances.* San Francisco, CA: Four Trees Publications, 1985.

Adamson, S. and Metzner, R. The nature of the MDMA experience and its role in healing, psychotherapy, and spiritual practice. *Revision*, 1988, 10:59-72.

Adler, J. Getting high on Ecstasy. *Newsweek*, 1985, 105:96.

Aguirre, N., Frechilla, D., Garcia-Ostra, A., Lasheras, B., and Del Rio, J. Differential regulation by methylenedioxymethamphetamine of 5-hydroxytryptamine1A receptor density and mRNA expression in rat hippocampus, frontal cortex, and brainstem: The role of corticosteroids. *Journal of Neurochemistry*, 1997, 68:1099-1105.

Aguirre, N., Galbete, J.L., Lasheras, B., and Del Rio, J. Methylenedioxymethamphetamine induces opposite changes in central pre- and postsynaptic 5-HT1A receptors in rats. *European Journal of Pharmacology*, 1995, 281:101-105.

Albery, N. Ecstasy—A drug for healing relationships? *Social Inventions*, 1988, 14:16-18.

Ali, S.F., Scallet, A.C., Newport, G.D., Lipe, G.W., Holson, R.R., and Slikker, W. Persistent neurochemical and structural changes in rat brain after oral administration of MDMA. *Research Communications in Substance Abuse*, 1989, 10:225-236.

Allen, R.P., McCann, U.D., and Ricaurte, G.A. Persistent effects of (+/-)3,4-methylenedioxymethamphetamine (MDMA, "Ecstasy") on human sleep. *Sleep*, 1993, 16:560-564.

Ames, D. and Wirshing, W.C. Ecstasy, the serotonin syndrome and neuroleptic malignant syndrome—A possible link? *Journal of the American Medical Association*, 1993, 269:869.

Anderson, G.M., Braun, G., Braun, U., Nichols, D.E., and Shulgin, A.T. Absolute configuration and psychomimetic activity. In G. Barnett, M. Trsic, and R. Willette (Eds.), *QuaSAR Research Monograph 22,* Washington, DC: National Institute on Drug Abuse, 1978.

Azmitia, E.C., Murphy, R.B., and Whitaker-Azmitia, P.M. MDMA (Ecstasy) effects on cultured serotonergic neurons: Evidence for Ca2+ dependent toxicity linked to release. *Brain Research*, 1990, 510:97-103.

Baker, L.E., Broadbent, J., Michael, E.K., and Matthews, P.K. Assessment of the discriminative stimulus effects of the optical isomers of Ecstasy (3,4-methylenedioxymethamphetamine; MDMA). *Behavioral Pharmacology*, 1995, 6:263-275.

Baker, L.E. and Makhay, M.M. Effects of (+)-fenfluramine on 3,4-methylene-dioxymethamphetamine discrimination in rats. *Pharmacology, Biochemistry, and Behavior*, 1996, 53:455-461.

Barnes, D.M. New data intensify the agony over Ecstasy. *Science*, 1988, 239:864-866.

Barrett, P.J. Ecstasy and dantrolene. *British Medical Journal*, 1992, 305:1225-1226.

Barrett, P.J. and Taylor, G.T. Ecstasy ingestion: A case report of severe complications. *Journal of the Royal Society of Medicine*, 1993, 86:233-234.

Battaglia, G., Brooks, B.P., Kulsakdinum, C., and De Souza, E.B. Pharmacologic profile of MDMA 3,4-methylenedioxymethamphetamine at various brain recognition sites. *European Journal of Pharmacology*, 1988, 149:159-163.

Battaglia, G. and De Souza, E.B. New perspectives on MDMA (3,4-methylene-dioxymethamphetamine). *Substance Abuse*, 1987, 8:31-42.

Battaglia, G., Sharkey, J., Kuhar, M.J., and De Souza, E.B. Neuroanatomic specificity and time course of alerations in rat brain serotonergic pathways induced by MDMA (3,4-methylenedioxymethamphetamine): Assessment using quantitative autoradiography. *Synapse*, 1991, 8:249-260.

Battaglia, G., Yeh, S.Y., O'Hearn, E., Molliver, M.E., Kuhar, M.J., and De Souza, E.B. 3,4-Methylenedioxymethamphetamine and 3,4-methylenedioxyampheta-mine destroy serotonin terminals in rat brain: Quantification of neurogeneration by measurements of [^{3}H] paroxetine-labelled serotonin uptake sites. *Journal of Pharmacology and Experimental Therapeutics*, 1987, 242:911-916.

Battaglia, G., Yeh, S.Y., and De Souza, E.B. MDMA-induced neurotoxicity: Parameters of degeneration and recovery of brain serotonin neurons. *Pharmacology, Biochemistry, and Behavior*, 1988, 29:269-274.

Battaglia, G., Zaczek, R., and De Souza, E.B. MDMA effects in brain: Pharmacologic profile and evidence of neurotoxicity from neurochemical and autoradiographic studies. In S.J. Peroutka (Ed.), *Ecstasy: The Clinical, Pharmacological, and Neurotoxicological Effects of the Drug MDMA*. Boston, MA: Kluwer Academic Publishers, 1990.

Baum, R. New variety of street drugs poses growing problem. *Chemical Engineering News*, 1985, 63:7-16.

Beardsley, P.M., Balster, R.L., and Harris, L.S. Self-administration of methylene-dioxymethamphetamine (MDMA) by rhesus monkeys. *Drug and Alcohol Dependence*, 1986, 18:149-157.

Beck, J. MDMA: The popularization and resultant implications of a recently controlled psychoactive substance. *Contemporary Drug Problems*, 1986, 13:305-313.

Beck, J. The public health implications of MDMA use. In S.J. Peroutka (Ed.), *Ecstasy: The Clinical, Pharmacological, and Neurotoxicological Effects of the Drug MDMA*. Boston, MA: Kluwer Academic Publishers, 1990.

Beck, J. and Morgan, P.A. Designer drug confusion: A focus on MDMA. *Journal of Drug Education*, 1986, 16:287-302.

Beck, J. and Rosenbaum, M. The scheduling of MDMA ("Ecstasy"). In J.A. Inciardi (Ed.), *Handbook of Drug Control in the United States*. Westport, CT: Greenwood Press, 1990.

Beck, J. and Rosenbaum, M. *Pursuit of Ecstasy: The MDMA Experience.* Albany, NY: SUNY Press, 1994.

Bedford-Russell, A.R., Schwartz, R.H., and Dawling, S. Accidental ingestion of Ecstasy. *Archives of Disease in Childhood*, 1992, 67:1114-1115.

Benazzi, F. and Mazzoli, M. Psychiatric illness associated with "Ecstasy." *Lancet*, 1991, 338:1520.

Bilsky, E.J., Hubbell, C.L., Delconte, J.D., and Reid, L.D. MDMA produces a conditioned place preference and elicits ejaculation in male rats: A modulatory role for the endogenous opioids. *Pharmacology, Biochemistry, and Behavior*, 1991, 40:443-447.

Bilsky, E.J., Hui, Y., Hubbell, C.L., and Reid, L.D. Methylenedioxymethamphetamine capacity to establish place preferences and modify intake of an alcohol beverage. *Pharmacology, Biochemistry, and Behavior*, 1990, 37:633-638.

Black, J., Farrell, M., and McGuire, P. Ecstasy in the brain: Unproven (but cause for concern) verdict on MDMA and brain damage. *Druglink*, 1992, 7:12-13.

Bost, R.O. 3,4-Methylenedioxymethamphetamine (MDMA) and other amphetamine derivatives. *Journal of Forensic Sciences*, 1988, 33:576-587.

Box, S.A., Prescott, L.F., and Freestone, S. Hyponatraemia at a rave. *Postgraduate Medical Journal*, 1997, 73:53-54.

Bradberry, C.W., Sprouse, J.S., Aghajanian, G.K., and Roth, R.H. 3,4-Methylenedioxymethamphetamine (MDMA)-induced release of endogenous serotonin from the rat dorsal raphe nucleus in vitro: Effects of fluoxetine and tryptophan. *Neurochemistry International*, 1990, 17:509-513.

Brady, J.F., Di Stefano, E.W., and Cho, A.K. Spectral and inhibitory interactions of (+/-)-3,4-methylenedioxyamphetamine (MDA) and (+/-)-3,4-methylenedioxymethamphetamine (MDMA) with rat hepatic microsomes. *Life Sciences*, 1986, 39:1457-1464.

Braun, U., Shulgin, A.T., and Braun, G. Centrally active N-substituted analogs of 3,4-methylenedioxyphenylisopropylamine (3,4-methylenedioxyamphetamine). *Journal of Pharmaceutical Sciences,* 1980, 69:192-195.

Britsch, A., Thiel, A., Rieckmann, P., and Prange, H. Acute inflammatory CNS disease after MDMA ("Ecstasy"). *European Neurology*, 1996, 36:328-329.

Broening, H.W., Bacon, L., and Slikker, W. Age modulates the long-term but not the acute effects of the serotonergic neurotoxicant 3,4-methylenedioxymethamphetamine. *Journal of Pharmacology and Experimental Therapeutics*, 1994, 271:285-293.

Broening, H.W., Bowyer, J.F., and Slikker, W. Age-dependent sensitivity of rats to the long-term effects of the serotonergic neurotoxicant (+/-)-3,4-methylenedioxymethamphetamine (MDMA) correlates with the magnitude of the MDMA-induced thermal response. *Journal of Pharmacology and Experimental Therapeutics*, 1995, 275:325-333.

Bronson, M.E., Barrios-Zambrano, L., Jiang, W., and Clark, C. Behavioral and developmental effects of two 3,4-methylenedioxymethamphetamine (MDMA) derivatives. *Drug and Alcohol Dependence*, 1994, 36:161-166.

Bronson, M.E., Wages, T.D., Beddingfield, T., and Horner, J.M. Morphine, MDMA, MDA and nexus produce a conditioned place preference in newly hatched chickens. *Experimental and Clinical Psychopharmacology*, 1996, 4:354-362.

Brown, C.R., McKinney, H., Osterloh, J.D., Shulgin, A.T., Jacob, P., and Olson, K.R. Severe adverse reaction to 3,4-methylenedioxymethamphetamine (MDMA). *Veterinary and Human Toxicology*, 1986, 28:490.

Brown, C.R. and Osterloh, J. Multiple severe complications from recreational ingestion of MDMA ("Ecstasy"). *Journal of the American Medical Association*, 1987, 258:780-781.

Brown, E.R.S., Jarvie, D.R., and Simpson, D. Use of drugs at "raves." *Scottish Medical Journal*, 1995, 40:168-171.

Bryden, A.A., Rothwell, P.J.N., and O'Reilly, P.H. Urinary retention with misuse of "Ecstasy." *British Medical Journal,* 1995, 310:504.

Buchanan, J. Ecstasy in the emergency department. *Clinical Toxicology Update*, 1985, 7:1-4.

Buffum, J. and Moser, C. MDMA and human sexual function. *Journal of Psychoactive Drugs*, 1986, 18:355-359.

Burnat, P., Le Brumant, P.C., Huart, B., Ceppa, F., and Pailler, F.M. Ecstasy: Psychostimulant, hallucinogen, and toxic substance. *Presse Medicale*, 1996, 25:1208-1212.

Burns, N., Olverman, H.J., Kelly, P.A., and Williams, B.C. Effects of Ecstasy on aldosterone secretion in the rat in vivo and in vitro. *Endocrine Research*, 1996, 22:601-606.

Cadet, J.L., Ladenheim, B., Baum, I., Carlson, E., and Epstein, C. CuZn-superoxide dismutase (CuZn SOD) transgenic mice show resistance to the lethal effects of methylenedioxyamphetamine (MDA) and of methylenedioxymethamphetamine (MDMA). *Brain Research*, 1994, 655:259-262.

Cadet, J.L., Ladenheim, B., Hirata, H., Rothman, R.B., Ali, S., Carlson, E., Epstein, C., and Moran, T.H. Superoxide radicals mediate the biochemical effects of methylenedioxymethamphetamine (MDMA): Evidence from using CuZn-superoxide dismutase transgenic mice. *Synapse*, 1995, 21:169-176.

Cadier, M.A. and Clarke, J.A. Ecstasy and whizz at a rave resulting in major burn plus complications. *Burns*, 1993, 19:239-240.

Callahan, P.M. and Appel, J.B. Differences in the stimulus properties of 3,4-methylenedioxyamphetamine and 3,4-methylenedioxymethamphetamine in animals trained to discriminate hallucinogens from saline. *Journal of Pharmacology and Experimental Therapeutics*, 1988, 246:866-870.

Callaway, C.W. and Geyer, M.A. Stimulant effects of 3,4-methylenedioxymethamphetamine in the nucleus accumbens of rat. *European Journal of Pharmacology*, 1992, 214:45-51.

Callaway, C.W. and Geyer, M.A. Tolerance and cross-tolerance to the activating effects of 3,4-methylenedioxymethamphetamine and a 5-hydroxytryptamine$_{1b}$ agonist. *Journal of Pharmacology and Experimental Therapeutics*, 1992, 263:318-326.

Callaway, C.W., Rempel, N., Peng, R.Y., and Geyer, M.A. Serotonin $5HT_1$-like receptors mediate hyperactivity in rats induced by 3,4-methylenedioxyme-thamphetamine. *Neuropsychopharmacology*, 1992, 7:113-127.

Callaway, C.W., Wing, L.L., and Geyer, M.A. Serotonin release contributes to the locomotor stimulant effects of 3,4-methylenedioxymethamphetamine in rats. *Journal of Pharmacology and Experimental Therapeutics*, 1990, 254:456-464.

Campkin, N.T.A. and Davies, U.M. Another death from Ecstasy. *Journal of the Royal Society of Medicine*, 1992, 85:61.

Cassidy, G. and Ballard, C.G. Psychiatric sequelae of MDMA (Ecstasy) and related drugs. *Irish Journal of Psychological Medicine*, 1994, 11:132-133.

Centini, F., Masti, A., and Barni, I.C. Quantitative and qualitative analysis of MDMA, MDEA, MA, and amphetamine in urine by headspace/solid phase micro-extraction (SPME) and GC/MS. *Forensic Science International*, 1996, 83:161-166.

Chadwick, I.S., Linsley, A., Freemont, A.J., Doran, B., and Curry, P.D. Ecstasy, 3,4-methylenedioxymethamphetamine (MDMA), a fatality associated with coagulopathy and hyperthermia. *Journal of the Royal Society of Medicine*, 1991, 84:371.

Che, S., Johnson, M., Hanson, G.R., and Gibb, J.W. Body temperature effect on methylenedioxymethamphetamine induced acute decrease in tryptophan hydroxy-lase activity. *European Journal of Pharmacology*, 1995, 293:445-453.

Cho, A.K., Hiramatsu, M., Di Stefano, E.W., Chang, A.S., and Jenden, D.J. Stereochemical differences in the metabolism of 3,4-methylenedioxymetham-phetamine in vivo and in vitro: A pharmacokinetic analysis. *Drug Metabolism and Disposition*, 1990, 18:686-691.

Chu, T., Kumagai, Y., Di Stefano, E.W., and Cho, A.K. Disposition of methylene-dioxymethamphetamine and three metabolites in the brains of different rat strains and their possible roles in acute serotonin depletion. *Biochemical Pharmacology*, 1996, 51:789-796.

Churchill, K.T. Identification of 3,4-methylenedioxymethamphetamine. *Microgram*, 1985, 18:123-132.

Climko, R.P., Roehrich, H., Sweeney, D.R., and Al-Razi, J. Ecstasy: A review of MDMA and MDA. *International Journal of Psychiatry in Medicine*, 1986-1987, 16:359-372.

Cohen, R.S. Subjective reports on the effects of the MDMA ("Ecstasy") experi-ence in humans. *Progress in Neuro-Psychopharmacology and Biological Psychiatry*, 1995, 19: 1137-1145.

Cohen, R.S. Adverse symptomatology and suicide associated with the use of methylenedioxymethamphetamine (MDMA; "Ecstasy"). *Biological Psychiatry*, 1996, 39:819-820.

Cohen, R.S. and Cocores, J. Neuropsychiatric manifestations following the use of 3,4-methylenedioxymethamphetamine (MDMA; "Ecstasy"). *Progress in Neuro-Psychopharmacology and Biological Psychiatry*, 1997, 21:727-734.

Cohen, S. They call it Ecstasy. *Drug Abuse and Alcoholism Newsletter*, 1985, XIV(6):1-3.

Colado, M.I. and Green, A.R. A study of the mechanism of MDMA ('Ecstasy')-induced neurotoxicity of 5-HT neurons using chlormethiazole, dizocilpine, and other protective compounds. *British Journal of Pharmacology*, 1994, 111:131-136.

Colado, M.I., Murray, T.K., and Green, A.R. 5-HT loss in rat brain following 3,4-methylenedioxymethamphetamine (MDMA), p-chloroamphetamine and fenfluramine administration and effects of chlormethiazole and dizocilpine. *British Journal of Pharmacology*, 1993, 108:583-589.

Colado, M.I., Williams, J.L., and Green, A.R. The hyperthermic and neurotoxic effects of "Ecstasy" (MDMA) and 3,4-methylenedioxyamphetamine (MDA) in the Dark Agouti (DA) rat, a model of the CYP2D6 poor metabolizer phenotype. *British Journal of Pharmacology*, 1995, 115:1281-1289.

Commins, D.L., Vosmer, G., Virus, R.M., Woolverton, C.R., Schuster, C.R., and Seiden, L.S. Biochemical and histological evidence that methylenedioxymethamphetamine (MDMA) is toxic to neurons in rat brain. *Journal of Pharmacology and Experimental Therapeutics*, 1987, 241:338-345.

Coore, J.R. A fatal trip with Ecstasy: A case of 3,4-methylenedioxymethamphetamine/3,4-methylenedioxyamphetamine toxicity. *Journal of the Royal Society of Medicine*, 1996, 89:51P-52P.

Cox, D.E. "Rave" to the grave. *Forensic Science International,* 1993, 60:5-6.

Cregg, M.T. and Tracey, J.A. Ecstasy abuse in Ireland. *Irish Medical Journal,* 1993, 86:118-120.

Creighton, F.J., Black, D.L., and Hyde, C.E. "Ecstasy" psychosis and flashbacks. *British Journal of Psychiatry,* 1991, 159:713-715.

Crifasi, J. and Long, C. Traffic fatality related to the use of methylenedioxymethamphetamine. *Journal of Forensic Sciences*, 1996, 41:1082-1084.

Crisp, T., Stafinsky, J.L., Boja, J.W., and Schechter, M.D. The antinociceptive effects of 3,4-methylenedioxymethamphetamine (MDMA) in the rat. *Pharmacology, Biochemistry, and Behavior*, 1989, 34:497-501.

Cuomo, M.J., Dyment, P.G., and Gammino, V.M. Increasing use of "Ecstasy" (MDMA) and other hallucinogens on a college campus. *Journal of American College Health*, 1994, 42:271-274.

Dafters, R.I. Effect of ambient temperature on hyperthermia and hyperkinesis induced by 3,4-methylenedioxymethamphetamine (MDMA or "Ecstasy") in rats. *Psychopharmacology*, 1994, 114:505-508.

Dafters, R.I. Hyperthermia following MDMA administration in rats: Effects of ambient temperature, water consumption, and chronic dosing. *Physiology and Behavior*, 1995, 58:877-882.

Dar, K.J. and McBrien, M.E. MDMA-induced hyperthermia: Report of a fatality and review of current therapy. *Intensive Care Medicine*, 1996, 22:995-996.

Davis, W.M., Hatoum, H.T., and Waters, I.W. Toxicity of MDA (3,4-methylenedioxyamphetamine considered for relevance to hazards of MDMA (Ecstasy) abuse. *Alcohol and Drug Research*, 1987, 7:123-134.

de la Fuente, H.L., Rodriguez-Arenas, M.A., Vicentre, O.J., Sanchez, P.J., and Barrio, A.G. Epidemiology of designer drug use in Spain. *Medicina Clinica,* 1997, 108:54-61.

de Man, R.A. Morbidity and mortality due to the use of Ecstasy. *Nederlands Tijdschrift voor Geneeskunde,* 1994, 138:1850-1855.

de Man, R.A., Wilson, J.H.P., and Tjen, H.S.L.M. Acuut leverfalen door methyleneendioxymetamfetamine. *Ned Tijdschr Geneeskd,* 1993, 137:727-729.

Demirkiran, M., Jankovic, J., and Dean, J.M. Ecstasy intoxication: An overlap between serotonin and neuroleptic malignant syndrome. *Clinical Neuropsychopharmacology,* 1996, 19:157-164.

Denborough, M.A. and Hopkinson, K.C. Dantrolene and "Ecstasy." *Medical Journal of Australia,* 1997, 166:165-166.

Docherty, J.P. Testimony on behalf of the Drug Enforcement Administration, United States Department of Justice, MDMA Aministrative Law Hearings, 1985, Docket No. 84-48.

Dornan, W.A., Katz, J.L., and Ricaurte, G.A. The effects of repeated administration of MDMA on the expression of sexual behavior in the male rat. *Pharmacology, Biochemistry, and Behavior,* 1991, 39:813-816.

Dowling, C.G. The trouble with Ecstasy. *Life Magazine,* 1985, 8:88-94.

Dowling, G.P. Human deaths and toxic reactions attributed to MDMA and MDEA. In S.J. Peroutka (Ed.), *Ecstasy: The Clinical, Pharmacological and Neurotoxicological Effects of the Drug MDMA.* Boston, MA: Kluwer Academic Publishers, 1990.

Dowling, G.P., McDonough, E.T., and Bost, R.O. "Eve" and "Ecstasy": A report of five deaths associated with the use of MDEA and MDMA. *Journal of the American Medical Association,* 1987, 257:1615-1617.

Downing, J. Testimony on behalf of Drs. Grinspoon and Greer, Professors Bakalar and Roberts, United States Department of Justice, MDMA Administrative Law Hearings, 1985, Docket No. 84-48.

Downing, J. The psychological and physiological effects of MDMA on normal volunteers. *Journal of Psychoactive Drugs,* 1986, 18:335-340.

Dowsett, R.P. Deaths attributed to an "Ecstasy" overdose. *Medical Journal of Australia,* 1996, 164:700.

Dupont, R.L. and Verebey, K. The role of the laboratory in the diagnosis of LSD and Ecstasy psychosis. *Psychiatric Annals,* 1994, 24:142-144.

Duxbury, A.J. Ecstasy: Dental implications. *British Dental Journal,* 1993, 175:38.

Dykhuizen, R.S., Brunt, P.W., Atkinson, P., Simpson, J.G., and Smith, C.C. Ecstasy induced hepatitis mimicking viral hepatitis. *Gut,* 1995, 36:939-941.

Ecstasy: Everything looks wonderful when you're young and on drugs. *Wet Magazine,* 1981, 9:76.

Ecstasy update. *Druglink,* 1996, 11:1.

Eichmeier, L.S. and Caplis, M.E. The forensic chemist: An "analytical detective." *Analytical Chemistry,* 1975, 47:841A-844A.

Eisner, B. *Ecstasy: The MDMA Story.* Berkeley, CA: Ronin, 1989.

Elk, C. MDMA (Ecstasy): Useful information for health professionals involved in drug education programs. *Journal of Drug Education*, 1996, 26:349-356.

Ellis, A.J., Wendon, J.A., Portmann, B., and Williams, R. Acute liver damage and Ecstasy ingestion. *Gut*, 1996, 38:454-458.

Ellis, P. and Schimmel, P. Ecstasy abuse. *New Zealand Medical Journal,* 1989, 102:358.

Ellis, S.J. Complications of "Ecstasy" misuse. *Lancet*, 1992, 340:726.

Evans, S.M. and Johanson, C.E. Discriminative stimulus properties of (+/-)-3,4-methylenedioxymethamphetamine and (+/-)-methylenedioxyamphetamine in pigeons. *Drug and Alcohol Dependence*, 1986, 18:159-164.

Fahal, I.H., Sallomi, D.F., Yaqoob, M., and Bell, G.M. Acute renal failure after Ecstasy. *British Medical Journal*, 1992, 305:29.

Farfel, G.M. and Seiden, L.S. Role of hypothermia in the mechanism of protection against serotonergic toxicity. I. Experiments using 3,4-methylenedioxymethamphetamine, dizocilpine, CGS 19755 and NBQX. *Journal of Pharmacology and Experimental Therapeutics*, 1995, 272:860-867.

Farfel, G.M., Vosmer, G.L., and Seiden, L.S. The n-methyl-d-aspartate MK-801 protects against serotonin depletions induced by methamphetamine, 3,4-methylenedioxymethamphetamine and p-chloroamphetamine. *Brain Research*, 1992, 595:121-127.

Farrell, M. Ecstasy and the oxygen of publicity. *British Journal of the Addictions*, 1989, 84:943.

Fernandez, P.L. MDMA (Ecstasy): A designer drug with high toxicity potential. *Anales de la Real Academia Nacional de Medicina*, 1994, 111:485-504.

Finch, E., Sell, L., and Arnold, D. Drug workers emphasize that water is not an antidote to drug (MDMA). *British Medical Journal*, 1996, 313:690.

Fineschi, V. and Masti, A. Fatal poisoning by MDMA (Ecstasy) and MDEA: A case report. *International Journal of Legal Medicine*, 1996, 108:272-275.

Finnegan, K.T., Ricaurte, G.A., Ritchie, L.D., Irwin, I., Peroutka, S.J., and Langston, J.W. Orally administered MDMA causes a long-term depletion of serotonin in rat brain. *Brain Research*, 1988, 447:141-144.

Fischer, C., Hatzidimitriou, G., Wlos, J., Katz, J., and Ricaurte, G.A. Reorganization of ascending 5-HT axon projections in animals previously exposed to the recreational drug (+/-)-3,4-methylenedioxymethamphetamine (MDMA, "Ecstasy"). *Journal of Neuroscience*, 1995, 15:5476-5485.

Fitzgerald, J. MDMA and harm. *International Journal of Drug Policy*, 1991, 2:22-24.

Fitzgerald, J.L. and Reid, J.J. Sympathomimetic actions of methylenedioxymethamphetamine in rat and rabbit cardiovascular tissues. *Journal of Pharmacy and Pharmacology*, 1994, 46:826-832.

Fitzgerald, R.L., Blanke, R.V., Glennon, R.A., Yousif, M.Y., Rosecrans, J.A., and Polkis, A. Determination of 3,4-methylenedioxyamphetamine and 3,4-methylenedioxymethamphetamine enantiomers in whole blood. *Journal of Chromatography*, 1989, 490:59-69.

Fitzgerald, R.L., Blanke, R.V., and Poklis, A. Stereoselective pharmacokinetics of 3,4-methylenedioxymethamphetamine in the rat. *Chirality*, 1990, 2:241-248.

Fitzgerald, R.L., Blanke, R.V., Rosecrans, J.A., and Glennon, R.A. Stereochemistry of the metabolism of MDMA to MDA. *Life Sciences*, 1989, 45:295-301.

Formyl derivatives of secondary bases. E. Merck. German Patent No. 334,555. *Chemical Abstracts*, 1923, 17:1803-1804.

Forrest, A.R.W., Galloway, J.H., Marsh, I.D., Strachan, G.A., and Clark, J.C. A fatal overdose with 3,4-methylenedioxyamphetamine derivatives. *Forensic Science International*, 1994, 64:57-59.

Frederick, D.L., Ali, S.F., Slikker, W., Gilliam, M.P., Allen, R.R., and Paule, M.G. Behavioral and neurochemical effects of chronic methylenedioxymethamphetamine (MDMA) treatment in rhesus monkeys. *Neurotoxicology and Teratology*, 1995, 17:531-543.

Frederick, D.L., Gilliam, M.P., Allen, R.R., and Paule, M. Acute effects of methylenedioxymethamphetamine (MDMA) on several complex brain functions in monkeys. *Pharmacology, Biochemistry, and Behavior*, 1995, 51:301-307.

Frederick, D.L. and Paule, M.G. Effects of MDMA on complex brain function in laboratory animals. *Neuroscience and Biobehavioral Reviews*, 1997, 21:67-78.

Frith, C.H., Chang, L.W., Lattin, D.L., Walls, R.C., Hamm, J., and Doblin, R. Toxicity of methylenedioxymethamphetamine (MDMA) in the dog and the rat. *Fundamental and Applied Toxicology*, 1987, 9:110-119.

Frombay, E. XTC: A new soft drug. *Tijdschrift voor Alcohol, Drugs en Andere Psychotrope Stoffen*, 1990, 16:150-158.

Frost, M., Kohler, H., and Blaschke, G. Analysis of "Ecstasy" by capillary electrophoresis. *International Journal of Legal Medicine*, 1996, 109:53-57.

Gallagher, W. MDMA: Is there ever a justifiable reason for getting high? *Discover*, 1986, 7:34.

Galloway, G., Shulgin, A.T., Kornfeld, H., and Frederick, S.L. Amphetamine, not MDMA, is associated with intracranial hemorrhage. *Journal of Accident and Emergency Medicine*, 1995, 12:231-232.

Gartside, S.E., McQuade, R., and Sharp, T. Effects of repeated administration of 3,4-methylenedioxymethamphetamine on 5-hydroxytryptamine neuronal activity and release in the rat brain in vivo. *Journal of Pharmacology and Experimental Therapeutics*, 1996, 279:277-283.

Gaston, T.R. and Rasmussen, G.T. Identification of 3,4-methylenedioxymethamphetamine. *Microgram*, 1972, 5:60-63.

Gaylor, D.W. and Slikker, W. Risk assessment for neurotoxic effects. *Neurotoxicology*, 1990, 11:211-218.

Gazzara, R.A., Takeda, H., Cho, A.K., and Howard, S.G. Inhibition of dopamine release by methylenedioxymethamphetamine is mediated by serotonin. *European Journal of Pharmacology*, 1989, 168:209-217.

Gehlert, D.R., Schmidt, C.J., Wu, L., and Lovenberg, W. Evidence for specific methylenedioxymethamphetamine (Ecstasy) binding sites in the rat brain. *European Journal of Pharmacology*, 1985, 119:135-136.

Gertz, K.R. "Hug Drug" alert: The agony of Ecstasy. *Harpers Bazaar*, 1985, 119:48, 46,263.

Gertz, K.R. The agony of Ecstasy. *Science Digest*, 1986, 94:27.

Gibb, J.W., Stone, D., Johnson, M., and Hanson, G.R. Neurochemical effects of MDMA. In S.J. Peroutka (Ed.), *Ecstasy: The Clinical, Pharmacological, and Neurotoxicological Effects of the Drug MDMA*. Boston, MA: Kluwer Academic Publishers, 1990.

Gifford, A.N., Minabe, Y., Toor, A., Wang, R.Y., and Ashby, C.R. Examination of the action of 3,4-methylenedioxymethamphetamine on rat A10 dopamine neurons. *Synapse*, 1996, 23:52-57.

Giroud, C., Augsburger, M., Sadeghipour, F., Varesio, E., Veuthey, J.L., and Rivier, L. Ecstasy—the status in French-speaking Switzerland. Composition of seized drugs, analysis of biological specimens, and short review of its pharmacological action and toxicity. *Schweizerische Rundschau fur Medizin Praxis*, 1997, 86:510-523.

Gledhill, J.A., Moore, D.F., Bell, D., and Henry, J.A. Subarachnoid haemorrhage associated with MDMA abuse. *Journal of Neurology, Neurosurgery, and Psychiatry*, 1993, 56:1036-1037.

Glennon, R.A., Little, P.J., Rosecrans, J.A., and Yousif, M. The effects of MDMA ("Ecstasy") and its optical isomers on schedule-controlled responding in mice. *Pharmacology, Biochemistry, and Behavior*, 1987, 26:425-426.

Glennon, R.A., Young, R., Rosecrans, J.A., and Anderson, G.M. Discriminative stimulus properties of MDA analogs. *Biological Psychiatry*, 1982, 17:807-814.

Goff, M.L., Miller, M.L., Paulson, J.D., Lord, W.D., Richards, E., and Omori, A.I. Effects of 3,4-methylenedioxymethamphetamine in decomposing tissues on the development of parasarcophaga ruficornis (Diptera Sarcophagida) and detection of the drug in postmortem blood, liver tissue, larvae, and puparia. *Journal of Forensic Sciences*, 1997, 42:276-280.

Gold, L.H., Hubner, C.B., and Koob, G.F. A role for the mesolimbic dopamine system in the psychostimulant actions of MDMA. *Psychopharmacology*, 1989, 99:40-47.

Gold, L.H. and Koob, G.F. Methysegide potentiates the hyperactivity produced by MDMA in rats. *Pharmacology, Biochemistry, and Behavior*, 1988, 29:645-648.

Gold, L.H. and Koob, G.F. MDMA produces stimulant-like conditioned locomotor activity. *Psychopharmacology*, 1989, 99:352-356.

Gold, L.H., Koob, G.F., and Geyer, M.A. Stimulant and hallucinogenic behavioral profiles 3,4-methylenedioxymethamphetamine and N-ethyl-3,4-methylenedioxyamphetamine in rats. *Journal of Pharmacology and Experimental Therapeutics*, 1988, 247:547-555.

Gollamudi, R., Ali, S.F., Lipe, G., Newport, G., Webb, P., Lopez, M., Leakey, J.E.A., Kolta, M., and Slikker, W. Influence of inducers and inhibitors on the metabolism in vitro and neurochemical effects in vivo of MDMA. *Neurotoxicology*, 1989, 10:455-466.

Gorard, D.A., Davies, S.E., and Clark, M.L. Misuse of Ecstasy. *British Medical Journal*, 1992, 305:309.

Gordon, C.J., Watkinson, W.P., O'Callaghan, J.P., and Miller, B.D. Effects of 3,4-methylenedioxymethamphetamine on autonomic thermoregulatory responses of the rat. *Pharmacology, Biochemistry, and Behavior*, 1991, 38:339-344.

Gough, B., Ali, S.F., Slikker, W., and Holson, R.R. Acute effects of 3,4-methylenedioxymethamphetamine (MDMA) on monoamines in rat. *Pharmacology, Biochemistry, and Behavior*, 1991, 39:619-623.

Gouzoulis-Mayfrank, E. and Hermle, L. The dangers of "Ecstasy." *Nervenarzt*, 1994, 64:648-650.

Gouzoulis-Mayfrank, E., Hermle, L., Kovar, K.A., and Sass, H. Entactogenic drugs "Ecstasy" (MDMA) and "Eve" (MDE) and other ring-substituted methamphetamine derivatives. A new class of substances among illegal drugs? *Nervenarzt*, 1996, 67:369-380.

Green, A.R., Cross, A.J., and Goodwin, G.M. Review of the pharmacology of 3,4-methylenedioxymethamphetamine (MDMA or "Ecstasy"). *Psychopharmacology*, 1995, 119:247-260.

Green, A.R. and Goodwin, G.M. Ecstasy and neurogeneration. *British Medical Journal*, 1996, 312:1493-1494.

Greer, G. MDMA: A new psychotropic compound and its effects in humans. privately published, 1983.

Greer, G. Testimony on behalf of Drs. Grinspoon and Greer, Professors Bakalar and Roberts, United States Department of Justice, MDMA Administrative Law Hearings, 1985, Docket No. 84-48.

Greer, G. Using MDMA in psychotherapy. *Advances*, 1985, 2:57-59.

Greer, G. Information on "Ecstasy." *American Journal of Psychiatry*, 1985, 142:1391.

Greer, G. Ecstasy and the dance of death. *British Medical Journal*, 1992, 305:775.

Greer, G. and Tolbert, R. Subjective reports of the effects of MDMA in a clinical setting. *Journal of Psychoactive Drugs*, 1986, 18:319-327.

Greer, G. and Tolbert, R. The therapeutic use of MDMA. In S.J. Peroutka (Ed.), *Ecstasy: The Clinical, Pharmacological, and Neurotoxicological Effects of the Drug MDMA*. Boston, MA: Kluwer Academic Publishers, 1990.

Grinspoon, L. Testimony on behalf of Drs. Grinspoon and Greer, Professors Bakalar and Roberts, United States Department of Justice, MDMA Administrative Law Hearings, 1985, Docket No. 84-48.

Grinspoon, L. and Bakalar, J.B. Can drugs be used to enhance the psychotherapeutic process. *American Journal of Psychotherapy*, 1986, XL:393-404.

Grob, C.S., Bravo, G., and Walsh, R. Second thoughts on 3,4-methylenedioxymethamphetamine (MDMA) neurotoxicity. *Archives of General Psychiatry*, 1990, 47:288-289.

Grob, C.S., Bravo, G.L., Walsh, R.N., and Liester, M.B. The MDMA-neurotoxicity controversy: Implications for clinical research with novel psychoactive drugs. *Journal of Nervous and Mental Disease*, 1992, 180:355-356.

Grob, C.S., Poland, R.E., Chang, L., and Ernst, T. Psychobiological effects of 3,4-methylenedioxymethamphetamine in humans: Methodological considerations and preliminary observations. *Behavioural Brain Research*, 1996, 73:103-107.

Grob, C.S. and Poland, R.E. MDMA. In J.H. Lowinson, P. Ruiz, R.B. Millman, and J.G. Langrod (Eds.), *Substance Abuse: A Comprehensive Textbook*. Baltimore, MD: Williams & Wilkins, 1997.

Gudelsky, G.A. Effect of ascorbate and cysteine on the 3,4-methylenedioxymethamphetamine induced depletion of brain serotonin. *Journal of Neural Transmission*, 1996, 103:1397-1404.

Gudelsky, G.A. and Nash, J.F. Carrier-mediated release of serotonin by 3,4-methylenedioxymethamphetamine: Implications for serotonin-dopamine interactions. *Journal of Neurochemistry*, 1996, 66:243-249.

Gudelsky, G.A., Yamamoto, B.K., and Nash, J.F. Potentiation of 3,4-methylenedioxymethamphetamine induced dopamine release and serotonin neurotoxicity by 5-HT2 receptor agonists. *European Journal of Pharmacology*, 1994, 264:325-330.

Hall, A.P., Lyburn, I.D., Spears, F.D., and Riley, B. An unusual case of Ecstasy poisoning. *Intensive Care Medicine*, 1996, 22:670-671.

Hanson, G.R., Merchant, K.M., Johnson, M., Letter, A.A., Bush, L., and Gibb, J.W. Effect of MDMA-like drugs on CNS neuropeptide systems. In S.J. Peroutka (Ed.), *Ecstasy: The Clinical, Pharmacological, and Neurotoxicological Effects of the Drug MDMA*. Boston, MA: Kluwer Academic Publishers, 1990.

Hansson, R.C. Clandestine laboratories: Production of MDMA 3,4-methylenedioxymethamphetamine. *Analog*, 1987, 9:1-10.

Hanyu, S., Kunihiko, I., Imai, H., Imai, N., and Yoshida, M. Cerebral infarction associated with 3,4-methylenedioxymethamphetamine ("Ecstasy") abuse. *European Neurology*, 1995, 35:173.

Hardman, H.F., Haavik, C.O., and Seevers, M.H. Relationship of the structure of mescaline and seven analogs to toxicity and behavior in five species of laboratory animals. *Toxicology and Applied Pharmacology*, 1973, 25:299-309.

Harries, D.P. and De Silva, R. "Ecstasy" and intracerebral haemorrhage. *Scottish Medical Journal*, 1992, 37:150-152.

Hashimoto, K. and Goromaru, T. Reduction of [^{3}H]6-nitroquipazine labelled 5-hydroxtryptamine uptake sites in rat brain by 3,4-methylenedioxymethamphetamine. *Fundamental and Clinical Pharmacology*, 1990, 4:635-641.

Hashimoto, K. and Goromaru, T. Reduction of in vivo binding of [^{3}H]paroxetine in mouse brain by 3,4-methylenedioxymethamphetamine. *Neuropharmacology*, 1990, 29:633-639.

Hashimoto, K. and Goromaru, T. Study of 3,4-methylenedioxymethamphetamine induced neurotoxicity in rat brain using specific in vivo binding of [^{3}H]6-nitroquipazine. *Research Communications in Substance Abuse*, 1992, 13:191-201.

Hayner, G.N. and McKinney, H. MDMA: The dark side of Ecstasy. *Journal of Psychoactive Drugs*, 1986, 18:341-347.

Hekmatpanah, C.R. and Peroutka, S.J. 5-Hydroxytryptamine uptake blockers attenuate the 5-hydroxytryptamine releasing effect of 3,4-methylenedioxymethamphetamine and related agents. *European Journal of Pharmacology*, 1990, 177:95-98.

Helmlin, H.J., Bracher, K., Bourquin, D., Von Lanthen, M., and Brenneisen, R. Analysis of 3,4-methylenedioxymethamphetamine (MDMA) and its metabolites in plasma and urine by HPLC-DAD and GC-MS. *Journal of Analytical Toxicology*, 1996, 20:432-440.

Henry, J.A. Ecstasy and the dance of death. *British Medical Journal*, 1992, 305:5-6.

Henry, J.A. Ecstasy and serotonin depletion. *Lancet*, 1996, 347:833.

Henry, J.A., Jeffreys, K.J., and Dawling, S. Toxicity and deaths from 3,4-methylenedioxymethamphetamine ("Ecstasy"). *Lancet*, 1992, 340:384-387.

Hewitt, K.E. and Green, A.R. Chlormethiazole, dizocilpine, and haloperidol prevent the degeneration of serotonergic nerve terminals induced by administration of MDMA ("Ecstasy") to rats. *Neuropharmacology*, 1994, 33:1589-1595.

Hiramatsu, M. and Cho, A.K. Enantiomeric differences in the effects of 3,4-methylenedioxymethamphetamine on extracellular monoamines and metabolites in the striatum of freely moving rats: An in vivo microdialysis study. *Neuropharmacology*, 1990, 29:269-275.

Hiramatsu, M., Kumugai, Y., Unger, S.E., and Cho, A.K. Metabolism of methylenedioxymethamphetamine: Formulation of dihydroxymethamphetamine and a quinone identified as its glutathione adduct. *Journal of Pharmacology and Experimental Therapeutics*, 1990, 254:521-527.

Hiramatsu, M., Di Stefano, E., Chang, A.S., and Cho, A.K. A pharmacokinetic analysis of 3,4-methylenedioxymethamphetamine effects on monoamine concentrations in brain dialysates. *European Journal of Pharmacology*, 1991, 204: 135-140.

Hiramatsu, M., Nabeshima, T., Kameyama, T., Maeda, Y., and Cho, AK. The effect of optical isomers of 3,4-methylenedioxymethamphetamine (MDMA) on stereotyped behavior in rats. *Pharmacology, Biochemistry, and Behavior*, 1989, 33:343-347.

Holden, R. and Jackson, M.A. Near-fatal hyponatraemic coma due to vasopressin oversecretion after "Ecstasy" (3,4-MDMA). *Lancet*, 1996, 347:1052.

Hooft, P.J. and van de Voorde, H.P. Reckless behavior related to the use of 3,4-methylenedioxymethamphetamine (Ecstasy). *International Journal of Legal Medicine*, 1994, 106:328-329.

House, R.V., Thomas, P.T., and Bhargava, H.N. Selective modulation of immune function resulting from in vitro exposure to methylenedioxymethamphetamine (Ecstasy). *Toxicology*, 1995, 96:59-69.

Huarte-Muniesa, M.P. and Pueyo Royo, A.M. Acute hepatitis due to ingestion of Ecstasy. *Revista Espanola de Enfermedades Digestivas*, 1995, 87:681-683.

Hubner, C.B., Bird, M., Rassnick, S., and Lornetsky, C. The threshold lowering effects of MDMA (Ecstasy) on brain-stimulating reward. *Psychopharmacology*, 1988, 95:49-51.

Huckle, P., Palmer, D., Lester, H., and Huws, D. Case report: "Ecstasy"—The road to psychosis? *British Journal of Clinical and Social Psychiatry*, 1991, 8:4-5.

Hughes, J.C., McCabe, M., and Evans, R.J. Intracranial haemorrhage with ingestion of "Ecstasy." *Archives of Emergency Medicine*, 1993, 10:372-374.

Ijzermans, J.N.M., Tilanus, H.W., de Man, R.A., and Metselaar, H.J. Ecstasy and liver transplantation. *Annales de Medecine Interne*, 1993, 144:568.

Ingrasci, R. Testimony on behalf of Drs. Grinspoon and Greer, Professors Bakalar and Roberts, United States Department of Justice, MDMA Administrative Law Hearings, 1985, Docket No. 84-48.

Insel, T.R., Battaglia, G.A., Johannessen, J.N., Marra, S., and De Souza, E.B. 3,4-Methylenedioxymethampetamine ("Ecstasy") selectively destroys brain serotonin terminals in rhesus monkeys. *Journal of Pharmacology and Experimental Therapeutics*, 1989, 249:713-720.

Johnson, M.P., Conarty, P.F., and Nichols, D.E. [^{3}H]Monoamine releasing and uptake inhibition properties of 3,4-methylenedioxymethamphetamine and p-chloroamphetamine analogues. *European Journal of Pharmacology*, 1991, 200:9-16.

Johnson, M.P., Hanson, G.R., and Gibb, J.W. Effects of dopaminergic and serotonergic receptor blockade on neurochemical changes induced by acute administration of methamphetamine and 3,4-methylenedioxymethamphetamine. *Neuropharmacology*, 1988, 27:1089-1096.

Johnson, M.P., Hanson, G.R., and Gibb, J.W. Effect of MK-801 on the decrease in tryptophan hydroxylase induced by methamphetamine and its methylenedioxy analog. *European Journal of Pharmacology*, 1989, 165:315-318.

Johnson, M.P., Hoffman, A.J., and Nichols, D.E. Effects of the enantiomers of MDA, MDMA, and related analogues on [^{3}H]serotonin and [^{3}H]dopamine release from superfused rat brain slices. *European Journal of Pharmacology*, 1986, 132:269-276.

Johnson, M.P., Huang, X., and Nichols, D.E. Serotonin neurotoxicity in rats after combined treatment with a dopaminergic agent followed by a non-neurotoxic 3,4-methylenedioxymethamphetamine (MDMA) analogue. *Pharmacology, Biochemistry, and Behavior*, 1991, 40:915-922.

Johnson, M.P., Mitros, K., Stone, D.M., Zobrist, R., Hanson, G.R., and Gibb, J.W. Effect of flunarizine and nimodipine on the decrease in tryptophan hydroxylase activity induced by methamphetamine and 3,4-methylenedioxymethamphetamine. *Journal of Pharmacology and Experimental Therapeutics*, 1992, 261:586-591.

Johnson, M.P. and Nichols, D.E. Neurotoxin effects of the alpha-ethyl homologue of MDMA following subacute administration. *Pharmacology, Biochemistry and Behavior*, 1989, 33:105-108.

Johnson, M.P. and Nichols, D.E. Combined administration of a non-neurotoxic 3,4-methylenedioxymethamphetamine analogue with amphetamine produces serotonin neurotoxicity in rats. *Neuropharmacology*, 1991, 30:819-822.

Johnson, M.P., Stone, D.M., Bush, L.G., Hanson, G.R., and Gibb, J.W. Glucocorticoid and 3,4-methylenedioxymethamphetamine (MDMA) induced neurotoxicity. *European Journal of Pharmacology*, 1989, 161:181.

Jones, C. and Dickinson, P. From Ecstasy to agony. *Nursing Times*, 1992, 88:27-30.

Kalix, P.A., Yousif, M.Y., and Glennon, R.A. Differential effects of the enantiomers of methylenedioxymethamphetamine (MDMA) on the release of radioactivity from (^{3}H)dopamine prelabeled rat striatum. *Research Communications in Substance Abuse*, 1988, 9:45-52.

Kamien, J.B., Johansen, C.E., Schuster, C.R., and Woolverton, W.L. The effects of (+/-)-methylenedioxymethamphetamine in monkeys trained to discriminate (+)-amphetamine from saline. *Drug and Alcohol Dependence*, 1986, 18:139-147.

Kaskey, G.B. Possible interaction between an MAOI and "Ecstasy." *American Journal of Psychiatry*, 1992, 149:411-412.

Keenan, E., Gervin, M., Dorman, A., and O'Connor, J.J. Psychosis and recreational use of MDMA. *Irish Journal of Psychological Medicine*, 1993, 10:162-163.

Kehne, J.H., Ketteler, H.J., McCloskey, T.C., Sullivan, C.K., Dudley, M.W., and Schmidt, C.J. Effects of the selective 5-HT$_{2a}$ receptor agonist MDL 100,907 on MDMA-induced locomotor stimulation in rats. *Neuropsychopharmacology*, 1996, 15:116-124.

Kehne, J.H., McCloskey, T.C., Taylor, V.L., Black, C.K., Fadayel, G.M., and Schmidt, C.J. Effects of the serotonin releasers methylenedioxymethamphetamine (MDMA), 4-chloroamphetamine (PCA), and fenfluramine on acoustic and tactile startle reflexes in rats. *Journal of Pharmacology and Experimental Therapeutics*, 1992, 260:78-89.

Kelland, M.D., Freeman, A.S., and Chiodo, L.A. (+/-)-3,4-methylenedioxymethamphetamine induced changes in the basal activity and pharmacological responsiveness of nigrostriatal dopamine neurons. *European Journal of Pharmacology*, 1989, 169:11-21.

Kessel, B. Hyponatraemia after ingestion of Ecstasy. *British Medical Journal*, 1994, 308:414.

Keup, W. MDMA—"Ecstasy." *Medizinische Monatsschrift fur Pharmazeuten*, 1996, 19:2-5.

Khakoo, S.I., Coles, C.J., Armstrong, J.S., and Barry, R.E. Hepatotoxicity and accelerated fibrosis following 3,4-methylenedioxymethamphetamine ("Ecstasy") usage. *Journal of Clinical Gastroenterology*, 1995, 20:244-247.

Kikura, R., Nakahara, Y., Mieczkowski, T., and Tagliaro, F. Hair analysis for drug abuse. XV. Disposition of 3,4-methylenedioxymethamphetamine (MDMA) and its related compounds into rat hair and application to hair analysis for MDMA abuse. *Forensic Science International*, 1997, 84:165-177.

Kirsch, M.M. *Designer Drugs*. Minneapolis, MN: Compcare, 1986.

Klein, J. The new drug they call Ecstasy: Is it too much to swallow? *New York Magazine*, 1985, 18:38-43.

Kleinman, J.E. Testimony on behalf of the Drug Enforcement Administration, United States Department of Justice, MDMA Aministrative Law Hearings, 1985, Docket No. 84-48.

Kleven, M.S., Woolverton, W.L., and Seiden, L.S. Evidence that both intragastric and subcutaneous administration of methylenedioxymethamphetamine (MDMA) produces serotonin neurotoxicity in rhesus monkeys. *Brain Research*, 1989, 488:121-125.

Klintz, P., Cirimele, V., Tracqui, A., and Mangin, P. Simultaneous determination of amphetamine, methamphetamine, 3,4-methylenedioxyamphetamine, and 3,4-methylenedioxymethamphetamine in human hair by gas chromatography-mass spectrometry. *Journal of Chromatography B-Biomedical Applications*, 1995, 670:162-166.

Kosten, T.R. and Price, L.H. Commentary: Phenomenology and sequelae of 3,4-methylenedioxymethamphetamine use. *Journal of Nervous and Mental Disease*, 1992, 180:353-354.

Kramer, H.K., Poblete, J.C., and Azmitia, E.C. 3,4-Methylenedioxymethamphetamine ("Ecstasy") promotes the translocation of protein kinase C (PKC): Requirement of viable serotonin nerve terminals. *Brain Research*, 1995, 680:1-8.

Krystal, J.H., Price, L.H., Opsahl, C., Ricaurte, G.A., and Heninger, G.R. Chronic 3,4-methylenedioxymethamphetamine (MDMA) use: Effects on mood and neuropsychological function? *American Journal of Drug and Alcohol Abuse*, 1992, 18:331-341.

Kuhlmann, T. Ecstasy, a new designer drug in the techno scene. *Psychiatrische Praxis*, 1996, 23:266-269.

Kulmala, H.K., Boja, J.W., and Schechter, M.D. Behavioral suppression following 3,4-methylenedioxymethamphetamine. *Life Sciences*, 1987, 41:1425-1429.

Kumagai, Y., Lin, L.Y., Schmitz, D.A., and Cho, A.K. Hydroxyl radical mediated demethylation of (methylenedioxy)phenyl compounds. *Chemical Research in Toxicology*, 1991, 4:330-334.

Kumagai, Y., Wickham, K.A., Schmitz, D.A., and Cho, A.K. Metabolism of methylenedioxyphenyl compounds by rabbit liver preparations. *Biochemical Pharmacology*, 1991, 42:1061-1067.

Kunsman, G.W., Levine, B., Kuhlman, J.J., Jones, R.L., Hugles, R.O., Fujiyama, C.I., and Smith, M.L. MDA-MDMA concentrations in urine specimens. *Journal of Analytical Toxicology*, 1996, 20:517-521.

Lamb, R.J. and Griffiths, R.R. Self-injection of dl,3,4-methylenedioxymethamphetamine in the baboon. *Psychopharmacology*, 1987, 91:268-272.

Larner, A.J. Complications of "Ecstasy" misuse. *Lancet*, 1992, 340:726.

Lawn, J.C. Schedules of controlled substances: Temporary placement of 3,4-methylenedioxymethamphetamine (MDMA) into Schedule I. *Federal Register*, 1985, 50:23,118-23,120.

Lawn, J.C. Schedules of controlled substances: Extension of temporary control of 3,4-methylenedioxymethamphetamine (MDMA) in Schedule I. *Federal Register*, 1986, 51:21,911-21,912.

Lawn, J.C. Schedules of controlled substances: Scheduling of 3,4-methylenedioxymethamphetamine (MDMA) into Schedule I of the Controlled Substances Act. *Federal Register*, 1986, 51:36,552-36,560.

Lawn, J.C. Schedules of controlled substances: Deletion of 3,4-methylenedioxy-methamphetamine (MDMA) from Schedule I of the Controlled Substances Act. *Federal Register*, 1988, 53:2225.

Lawn, J.C. Schedules of controlled substances: Scheduling of 3,4-methylenedioxy-ymethamphetamine (MDMA) into Schedule I of the Controlled Substances Act, Remand. *Federal Register*, 1988, 53:5156.

Le Sage, M., Clark, R., and Poling, A. MDMA and memory: The acute and chronic effects of MDMA in pigeons performing under a delayed-matching-to-sample procedure. *Psychopharmacology*, 1993, 110:327-332.

Lee, J.W. Catatonic stupor after "Ecstasy." *British Medical Journal*, 1994, 308:717-718.

Lehane, M. and Rees, C. When Ecstasy means agony. *Nursing Standard*, 1996, 10:24-25.

Lehmann, E., Thom, C.H., and Croft, D.N. Delayed severe rhabdomyolysis after taking "Ecstasy." *Postgraduate Medical Journal,* 1995, 71:186-187.

Leonardi, E.T. and Azmitia, E.C. MDMA (Ecstasy) inhibition of MAO type A and type B: Comparisons with fenfluramine and fluoxetine (Prozac). *Neuropsychopharmacology*, 1994, 10:231-238.

Leverant, R. MDMA reconsidered. *Journal of Psychoactive Drugs*, 1986, 18:373-379.

Levine, A.J., Rees, G.M., and Drew, S. "Ecstasy" induced pneumomediastinum. *Journal of the Royal Society of Medicine*, 1993, 86:232-233.

Lew, R., Sabol, K.E., Chou, C., Vosmer, G.L., Richards, J., and Seiden, L.S. Methylenedioxymethamphetamine-induced serotonin deficits are followed by partial recovery over a 52-week period. Part II: Radioligand binding and autoradiography studies. *Journal of Pharmacology and Experimental Therapeutics*, 1996, 276:855-865.

Li, A.A., Marek, G.J., Vosmer, G., and Seiden, L.S. Long-term central 5-HT depletions resulting from repeated administration of MDMA enhances the effects of single administration of MDMA on schedule-controlled behavior of rats. *Pharmacology, Biochemistry, and Behavior*, 1989, 33:641-648.

Liester, M.B., Grob, C.S., Bravo, G.L., and Walsh, R.N. Phenomenology and sequelae of 3,4-methylenedioxymethamphetamine use. *Journal of Nervous and Mental Disease*, 1992, 180:345-352.

Lim, H.K. and Foltz, R.L. In vivo and in vitro metabolism of 3,4-methylenedioxy-methamphetamine in the rat: Identification of metabolites using an ion trap detector. *Chemical Research in Toxicology*, 1988, 1:370-378.

Lim, H.K. and Foltz, R.L. Identification of metabolites of 3,4-methylenedioxyme-thamphetamine in human urine. *Chemical Research in Toxicology*, 1989, 2:142-143.

Lim, H.K. and Foltz, R.L. In vivo formation of aromatic hydroxylated metabolites of 3,4-methylenedioxymethamphetamine in the rat: Identification by ion trap tandem mass spectrometric (MS/MS and MS/MS/MS) techniques. *Biological Mass Spectrometry*, 1991, 20:677-686.

Lin, H.Q., Jackson, D.M., Atrens, D.M., Christie, M.J., and McGregor, I.S. Serotonergic modulation of 3,4-methylenedioxymethamphetamine (MDMA)-elicited reduction of response rate but not rewarding threshold in accumbal self-stimulation. *Brain Research*, 1997, 744:351-357.

Lin, L., Kumagai, Y., and Cho, A.K. Enzymatic and chemical demethylation of (methylenedioxy)amphetamine and (methylenedioxy)methamphetamine by rat brain microsomes. *Chemical Research in Toxicology*, 1992, 5:401-406.

Lin, H.Q., McGregor, I.S., Atrens, D.M., and Christie, M. Contrasting effects of dopaminergic blockade on MDMA and d-amphetamine. *Pharmacology, Biochemistry, and Behavior*, 1994, 47:369-374.

Logan, B.J., Laverty, R., Sanderson, W.D., and Yee, Y.B. Differences between rats and mice in MDMA (methylenedioxymethamphetamine) neurotoxicity. *European Journal of Pharmacology*, 1988, 152:227-234.

Logan, A., Stickle, B., O'Keefe, N., and Hewitson, H. Survival following "Ecstasy" ingestion with a peak temperature of 42°C. *Anaesthesia*, 1993, 48:1017-1018.

Lynch, R. Testimony on behalf of Drs. Grinspoon and Greer, Professors Bakalar and Roberts, United States Department of Justice, MDMA Administrative Law Hearings, 1985, Docket No. 84-48.

Lyon, R.A., Glennon, R.A., and Titeler, M. 3,4-Methylenedioxymethamphetamine (MDMA): Stereoselective interactions at brain 5-HT$_1$ and 5-HT$_2$ receptors. *Psychopharmacology*, 1986, 88:525-526.

Malberg, J.E., Sabol, K.E., and Seiden, L.S. Co-administration of MDMA with drugs that protect against MDMA neurotoxicity produces different effects on body temperature in the rat. *Journal of Pharmacology and Experimental Therapeutics*, 1996, 278:258-267.

Manchanda, S. and Connolly, M.J. Cerebral infarction in association with Ecstasy abuse. *Postgraduate Medical Journal*, 1993, 69:874-875.

Mannaerts, G.H., Luitse, J.S., Zandstra, D.F., and Hoitsma, H.F. Morbidity and mortality due to the use of Ecstasy. *Nederlands Tijdschrift Voor Geneeskunde*, 1994, 138:2368.

Marona-Lewicka, D., Rhee, G.S., Sprague, J.E., and Nichols, D. Reinforcing effects of certain serotonin-releasing amphetamine derivatives. *Pharmacology, Biochemistry, and Behavior*, 1996, 53:99-105.

Marsh, J.C.W., Abboudi, Z.H., Gibson, F.M., Scopes, J., Daly, S., O'Shaunnessy, D.F.O., Baughan, A.S.J., and Gordon-Smith, E.C. Aplastic anaemia following exposure to 3,4-methylenedioxymethamphetamine ("Ecstasy"). *British Journal of Haematology*, 1994, 88:281-285.

Matthai, S.M., Sills, J.A., Davidson, D.C., and Alexandrou, D. Cerebral oedema after ingestion of MDMA and unrestricted intake of water. *British Medical Journal*, 1996, 312:1359.

Matthews, R.T., Champney, T.H., and Frye, G.D. Effects of (+/-)-methylenedioxymethamphetamine (MDMA) on brain dopaminergic activity in rats. *Pharmacology, Biochemistry, and Behavior*, 1989, 33:741-747.

Maxwell, D.L., Polkey, M.I., and Henry, J.A. Hyponatraemia and catatonic stupor after taking "Ecstasy." *British Medical Journal*, 1993, 307:1399.

McCann, U.D. MDMA: Is there cause for concern? In M.W. Fischman (Chair), *Hallucinogens, LSD, and Raves.* Symposium conducted at the National Press Club, Washington, DC, 1993.

McCann, U.D. and Ricaurte, G.A. Lasting neuropsychiatric sequelae of methylenedioxymethamphetamine ("Ecstasy") in recreational users. *Journal of Clinical Psychopharmacology,* 1991, 11:302-305.

McCann, U.D. and Ricaurte, G.A. MDMA ("Ecstasy") and panic disorder: Induction by a single dose. *Biological Psychiatry,* 1992, 32:950-953.

McCann, U.D. and Ricaurte, G.A. Reinforcing subjective effects of (+/-) 3,4-methylenedioxymethamphetamine ("Ecstasy") may be separable from its neurotoxic actions: Clinical evidence. *Journal of Clinical Psychopharmacology,* 1993, 13:214-217.

McCann, U.D. and Ricaurte, G.A. On the neurotoxity of MDMA and related amphetamine derivatives. *Journal of Clinical Psychopharmacology,* 1995, 15:295-296.

McCann, U.D., Ridenour, A., Shaham, Y., and Ricaurte, G.A. Serotonin neurotoxicity after (+/-)3,4-methylenedioxymethamphetamine (MDMA; "Ecstasy"): A controlled study in humans. *Neuropsychopharmacology,* 1994, 10:129-138.

McCann, U.D., Slate, S.O., and Ricaurte, G.A. Adverse reactions with 3,4-methylenedioxymethamphetamine (MDMA; "Ecstasy"). *Drug Safety,* 1996, 15:107-115.

McCauley, J.C. Deaths attributed to an "Ecstasy" overdose. *Medical Journal of Australia,* 1996, 164:56.

McCormick, M. *Designer Drug Abuse.* New York: Franklin Watts, 1989.

McCoy, E.P., Renfrew, C., Johnston, J.R., and Lavery, G. Malignant hyperpyrexia in an MDMA ("Ecstasy") abuser. *The Ulster Medical Journal,* 1994, 63:103-107.

McDermott, P. MDMA use in the North West of England. *International Journal of Drug Policy,* 1993, 4:210-221.

McDowell, D. Ecstasy and raves: The '90s party scene. In M.W. Fischman (Chair), *Hallucinogens, LSD, and Raves.* Symposium conducted at the National Press Club, Washington DC, 1993.

McDowell, D.M. and Kleber, H.D. MDMA: Its history and pharmacology. *Psychiatric Annals,* 1994, 24:127-130.

McGuire, P., Cope, H., and Fahy, T.A. Diversity of psychopathology associated with use of 3,4-methylenedioxymethamphetamine ("Ecstasy"). *British Journal of Psychiatry,* 1994, 165:391-395.

McGuire, P. and Fahy, T. Chronic paranoid psychosis after misuse of MDMA ("Ecstasy"). *British Medical Journal,* 1991, 302:697.

McKenna, D.J. and Peroutka, S.J. The neurochemistry and neurotoxicity of 3,4-methylenedioxymethamphetamine (MDMA, "Ecstasy"). *Journal of Neurochemistry,* 1990, 54:14-22.

McNamara, M.G., Kelly, J.P., and Leonard, B.E. Some behavioral and neurochemical aspects of subacute (+/-)-3,4-methylenedioxymethamphetamine in rats. *Pharmacology, Biochemistry, and Behavior,* 1995, 52:479-484.

Meehan, S.M., Gordon, T.L., and Schechter, M.D. MDMA (Ecstasy) substitutes for the ethanol discriminative cue in HAD but not LAD rats. *Alcohol*, 1995, 12:569-572.

Merrill, J. Ecstasy and neurodegeneration. Advice is that "less is more." *British Medical Journal*, 1996, 313:423.

Metzner, R. The great entactogen-empathogen debate. *MAPS Newsletter*, 1993, IV(2):48-49.

Michel, R.E., Rege, A.B., and George, W.J. High pressure liquid chromatography/electrochemical detection method for monitoring MDA and MDMA in whole blood and other biological tissues. *Journal of Neuroscience Methods*, 1993, 50:61-66.

Miczek, K.A. and Haney, M. Psychomotor stimulant effects of d-amphetamine, MDMA and PCP: Aggressive and schedule-controlled behavior in mice. *Psychopharmacology*, 1994, 115:358-365.

Millan, M.J. and Colpaert, F.C. Methylenedioxymethamphetamine induces spontaneous tail flicks in the rat via 5-HT$_{1a}$ receptors. *European Journal of Pharmacology*, 1991, 193:145-152.

Miller, D.B. and O'Callaghan, J.P. The role of temperature, stress, and other factors in the neurotoxicity of the substituted amphetamines 3,4-methylenedioxymethamphetamine and fenfluramine. *Molecular Neurobiology*, 1995, 11:177-192.

Miller, N.S. and Gold, M.S. LSD and Ecstasy: Pharmacology, phenomenology, and treatment. *Psychiatric Annals*, 1994, 24:131-133.

Millman, R.B. and Beeder, A.B. The new psychedelic culture: LSD, Ecstasy, "rave" parties, and the Grateful Dead. *Psychiatric Annals*, 1994, 24:148-150.

Milroy, C.M., Clark, J.C., and Forrest, A.R.W. Pathology of deaths associated with "Ecstasy" and "Eve" misuse. *Journal of Clinical Pathology*, 1996, 49:149-153.

Mokler, D.J., Robinson, S.E., and Rosecrans, J.A. (+/-)-3,4-methylenedioxymethamphetamine (MDMA) produces long-term reductions in brain 5-hydroxytryptamine in rats. *European Journal of Pharmacology*, 1987, 138:265-268.

Moller-Nehring, E. and Luderer, H.J. Is the anxiety about Ecstasy justified? *Fortschritte der Medizin*, 1997, 115:28-34.

Montgomery, H. and Myerson, S. 3,4-Methylenedioxymethamphetamine (MDMA, or "Ecstasy") and associated hypoglycemia. *American Journal of Emergency Medicine*, 1997, 15:218.

Moore, K.A., Mozayani, A., Fierro, M.F., and Polkis, A. Distribution of 3,4-methylenedioxymethamphetamine (MDMA) and 3,4-methylenedioxyamphetamine (MDA) stereoisomers in a fatal poisoning. *Forensic Science International*, 1996, 83:111-119.

Mullen, F.M. Schedules of controlled substances: Proposed placement of 3,4-methylenedioxymethamphetamine into Schedule I. *Federal Register*, 1984, 49:30,210.

Mullen, F.M. Schedules of controlled substances; Proposed placement of 3,4-methylenedioxymethamphetamine into Schedule I. *Federal Register*, 1984, 49:732-733.

Murthy, B.V., Wilkes, R.G., and Roberts, N.B. Creatine kinase isoform changes following Ecstasy overdose. *Anaesthesia and Intensive Care*, 1997, 25:156-159.

Nader, M.A., Hoffmann, S.M., and Barrett, J.E. Behavioral effects of (+/-)-methylenedioxyamphetamine (MDA) and (+/-)-methylenedioxymethamphetamine (MDMA) in the pigeon: Interactions with noradrenergic and serotonergic systems. *Psychopharmacology*, 1989, 98:183-188.

Nash, J.F. Ketanserin pretreatment attenuates MDMA-induced dopamine release in the striatum as measured by in vivo microdialysis. *Life Sciences,* 1990, 47:2401-2408.

Nash, J.F. and Brodkin, J. Microdialysis studies on 3,4-methylenedioxymethamphetamine-induced dopamine release: Effect of dopamine uptake inhibitors. *Journal of Pharmacology and Experimental Therapeutics*, 1991, 259:820-825.

Nash, J.F., Roth, B.L., Brodkin, J.D., Nichols, D.E., and Gudelsky, G.A. Effect of the R(-) and S(+) isomers of MDA and MDMA on phosphatidyl inositol turnover in cultured cells expressing 5-HT2A or 5-HT2C receptors. *Neuroscience Letters*, 1994, 177:111-115.

Nash, J.F. and Yamamoto, B.K. Methamphetamine neurotoxicity and striatal glutamate release: Comparison to 3,4-methylenedioxymethamphetamine. *Brain Research*, 1992, 581:237-243.

Nasmyth, P. The agony and the Ecstasy. *Face*, 1986, 78:53-55.

Nasmyth, P. Laing on Ecstasy. *International Journal of Drug Policy*, 1989, 1:14-15.

Nencini, P., Woolverton, W.L., and Seiden, L.S. Enhancement of morphine-induced analgesia after repeated injections of methylenedioxymethamphetamine. *Brain Research*, 1988, 457:136-142.

Newcombe, R. Ecstasy: New drug, familiar panic. *Mersey Drug Journal*, 1988, 2:12-13.

Newmeyer, J.A. Some considerations on the prevalence of MDMA use. *Journal of Psychoactive Drugs*, 1986, 18:361-362.

Newmeyer, J.A. X at the crossroads. *Journal of Psychoactive Drugs*, 1993, 25:341-342.

Nichols, D.E. Differences between the mechanism of action of MDMA, MBDB, and the classic hallucinogens: Identification of a new therapeutic class: Entactogens. *Journal of Psychoactive Drugs*, 1986, 18:305-313.

Nichols, D.E. The great entactogen-empathogen debate. *MAPS Newsletter*, 1993, IV(2):47.

Nichols, D.E., Danuta, M.L., Xuemei, H., and Johnson, M.P. Novel serotonergic agents. *Drug Design and Discovery*, 1993, 9:299-312.

Nichols, D.E. and Glennon, R.A. Medicinal chemistry and structure-activity relationships of hallucinogens. In B.L. Jacobs (Ed.), *Hallucinogens: Neurochemical, Behavioral, and Clinical Perspectives*. New York: Raven Press, 1984.

Nichols, D.E., Hoffman, A.J., Oberlender, R.A., Jacob, P., and Shulgin, A.T. Derivatives of 1-(1,3-benzodioxol-5-yl)-2-butanamine: Representatives of a novel therapeutic class. *Journal of Medicinal Chemistry*, 1986, 29:2009-2015.

Nichols, D.E., Lloyd, D.H., Hoffman, A.J., Nichols, M.B., and Yim, G.K.W. Effects of certain hallucinogenic amphetamine analogues on the release of [^{3}H]serotonin from rat brain synaptosomes. *Journal of Medicinal Chemistry*, 1982, 25:530-535.

Nichols, D.E. and Oberlender, R. Structure-activity relationships of MDMA and related compounds: A new class of psychoactive drugs? *Annals of the New York Academy of Sciences*, 1990, 600:613-625.

Nichols, D.E. and Oberlender, R. Structure-activity relationships of MDMA and related compounds: A new class of psychoactive agents? In S.J. Peroutka (Ed.), *Ecstasy: The clinical, pharmacological, and neurotoxicological effects of the drug MDMA*. Boston, MA: Kluwer Academic Publishers, 1990.

Nichols, D.E., Oberlender, R., Burris, K., Hoffman, A.J., and Johnson, M.P. Studies of dioxole ring substituted 3,4-methylenedioxyamphetamine (MDA) analogues. *Pharmacology, Biochemistry, and Behavior*, 1989, 34:571-576.

Nielson, J.C., Nicholson, K., Pitzner-Jorgensen, B.L., and Unden, M. Abuse of Ecstasy (3,4-methylenedioxymethamphetamine): Pharmacological, neuropsychiatric, and behavioral aspects. *Ugeskrift for Laeger*, 1995, 157:724-727.

Noggle, F.T., Clark, C.R., and DeRuiter, J. Liquid chromatographic and spectral methods for the differentiation of 3,4-methylenedioxymethamphetamine (MDMA) from regioisomeric phenethylamines. *Journal of Liquid Chromatography*, 1991, 14:913-918.

Noggle, F.T., Clark, C.R., and DeRuiter, J. Gas chromatographic and mass spectrometric analysis of samples from a clandestine laboratory involved in the synthesis of Ecstasy from sassafras oil. *Journal of Chromatographic Science*, 1991, 29:168-173.

Nuvials, X., Masclans, J.R., Peracaula, R., and de Latorre, F.J. Hyponatraemic coma after Ecstasy ingestion. *Intensive Care Medicine*, 1997, 23:480.

Oberlender, R. and Nichols, D.E. Drug discrimination studies with MDMA and amphetamine. *Psychopharmacology*, 1988, 95:71-76.

Oberlender, R. and Nichols, D.E. (+)-N-methyl-1-(1,3-benzo-dioxol-5-yl)-2-butanamine as a discriminative stimulus in studies of 3,4-methylenedioxymethamphetamine-like behavioral activity. *Journal of Pharmacology and Experimental Therapeutics*, 1990, 255:1098-1106.

Obradovic, T., Imel, K.M., and White, S.R. Methylenedioxymethamphetamine induced inhibition of neuronal firing in the nucleus accumbens is mediated by both serotonin and dopamine. *Neuroscience*, 1996, 74:469-481.

O'Connor, B. Hazards associated with the recreational drug "Ecstasy." *British Journal of Hospital Medicine*, 1994, 52:510-514.

O'Hearn, E., Battaglia, G., De Souza, E.B., Kuhar, M.J., and Molliver, M.E. Methylenedioxyamphetamine (MDA) and methylenedioxymethamphetamine (MDMA) cause selective ablation of serotonergic axon terminals in forebrain:

Immunocytochemical evidence for neurotoxicity. *Neuroscience,* 1988, 8:2788-2803.

O'Koon, M. Dangerous new drugs (Speed and Ecstasy). *Good Housekeeping,* 1989, 208:235-236.

Onwudike, M. Ecstasy induced retropharyngeal emphysema. *Journal of Accident and Emergency Medicine,* 1996, 13:359-361.

Oranje, W.A., von Pol, P., Wurff, A., Zeijen, R.N., Stockbrugger, R.W., and Arends, J.W. XTC-induced hepatitis. *Netherlands Journal of Medicine,* 1994, 44:56-59.

Padkin, A. Treating MDMA ("Ecstasy") toxicity. *Anaesthesia,* 1994, 49:259.

Pallanti, S. and Mazzi, D. MDMA (Ecstasy) precipitation of panic disorder. *Biological Psychiatry,* 1992, 32:91-95.

Pan, H.S. and Wang, R.Y. MDMA: Further evidence that its actions in the medial prefrontal cortex is mediated by the serotonergic system. *Brain Research,* 1991, 539:332-336.

Pan, H.S. and Wang, R.Y. The action of (+/-)-MDMA on medial prefrontal cortical neurons is mediated through the serotonergic system. *Brain Research,* 1991, 543:56-60.

Paris, J.M. and Cunningham, K.A. Lack of serotonin neurotoxicity after intra-raphe microinjection of (+/-)3,4-methylenedioxymethamphetamine (MDMA). *Brain Research Bulletin,* 1991, 28:115-119.

Parr, M.J., Low, H.M., and Botterill, P. Hyponatraemia and death after "Ecstasy" ingestion. *Medical Journal of Australia,* 1997, 166:136-137.

Pascual, B.S., Sarrion, M.J.V., Garcia, H.A., and Berenguer, L.J. Hepatitis and Ecstasy. *Medicina Clinica,* 1997, 108:279.

Patentschrift. *Verfahren zur Darstellung von Alkyloxyaryl-, Dialkyloxyaryl- und Alkylenedioxy-arylaminopropanen bzw. deren am Stickstoff monoalkylierten Derivaten.* Firma E. Merck in Darmstadt, Germany, 1914.

Paulus, M.P. and Geyer, M.A. The effects of MDMA and other methylenedioxy-substituted phenylalkylamines on the structure of rat locomotor activity. *Neuropsychopharmacology,* 1992, 7:15-31.

Pearson, G., Ditton, J., Newcombe, R., and Gilman, M. Everything starts with an "E": An introduction to Ecstasy use by young people in Britain. *Druglink,* 1991, 6:10-11.

Peroutka, S.J. Incidence of recreational use of 3,4-methylenedioxymethamphetamine (MDMA; "Ecstasy") on an undergraduate campus. *New England Journal of Medicine,* 1987, 317:1542-1543.

Peroutka, S.J. Relative insensitivity of mice to 3,4-methylenedioxymethamphetamine (MDMA) neurotoxicity. *Research Communications in Substance Abuse,* 1988, 9:193-206.

Peroutka, S.J. "Ecstasy": A human neurotoxin? *Archives of General Psychiatry,* 1989, 46:191.

Peroutka, S.J. Recreational use of MDMA. In S.J. Peroutka (Ed.), *Ecstasy: The Clinical, Pharmacological, and Neurotoxicological Effects of the Drug MDMA.* Boston, MA: Kluwer Academic Publishers, 1990.

Peroutka, S.J., Newman, H., and Harris, H. Subjective effects of 3,4-methylene-dioxymethamphetamine in recreational users. *Neuropsychopharmacology*, 1988, 1:273-277.

Peroutka, S.J., Pascoe, N., and Faull, K.F. Monoamine metabolites in the cerebrospinal fluid of recreational users of 3,4-methylenedioxymethamphetamine (MDMA, "Ecstasy"). *Research Communications in Substance Abuse*, 1987, 8:125-138.

Piercey, M.F., Lum, J.T., and Palmer, J.R. Effects of MDMA ("Ecstasy") on firing rates of serotonergic, dopaminergic and noradrenergic neurons in the rat. *Brain Research*, 1990, 526:203-206.

Platt, S. Moral panic. *New Statesman and Society.* November 24, 1995. Sec. Drugs:14-15.

Poland, R.E. Diminished corticotropin and enhanced prolactin responses to 8-hydroxy-2-(di-n-propyl-amino)tetralin in methylenedioxymethamphetamine pretreated rats. *Neuropharmacology*, 1990, 29:1099-1101.

Polkis, A., Fitzgerald, R.L., Hall, K.V., and Saady, J.J. Emit-d.a.u. monoclonal amphetamine/methamphetamine assay. II. Detection of methylenedioxyamphetamine (MDA) and methylenedioxymethamphetamine (MDMA). *Forensic Science International*, 1993, 59:63-70.

Prada, C. and Alvarez, F.J. MDMA or Ecstasy: Pharmacological, toxicological, and clinical aspects. *Medicina Clinica*, 1996, 107:549-555.

Prasad, N., Cargill, R., Wheeldon, N.M., Lang, C.C., and MacDonald, T.M. "Ecstasy" and meningococcal meningitis. *Infectious Diseases in Clinical Practice*, 1994, 3:122-124.

Prat, A., Montero, M., Reig, R., and Sanz, P. MDMA (Ecstasy): Todays drug in Spain. *Revista Clinica Espanola*, 1991, 188:106-108.

Premkumar, L.S. and Ahern, G.P. Blockade of a resting potassium channel and modulation of synaptic transmission by Ecstasy in the hippocampus. *Journal of Pharmacology and Experimental Therapeutics*, 1995, 274:718-722.

Price, L.H., Ricaurte, G.A., Krystal, J.H., and Heninger, G.R. Neuroendocrine and mood responses to intravenous L-tryptophan in 3,4-methylenedioxymethamphetamine (MDMA) users: Preliminary Observations. *Archives of General Psychiatry*, 1989, 46:20-22.

Priori, A., Bertolasi, L., Berardelli, A., and Mantredi, M. Acute dystonic reaction to Ecstasy. *Movement Disorders*, 1995, 10:353.

Randall, T. Ecstasy-fueled "rave" parties become dances of death for English youths. *Journal of the American Medical Association*, 1992, 268:1505-1506.

Randall, T. "Rave" scene, Ecstasy use, leap Atlantic. *Journal of the American Medical Association*, 1992, 268:1506.

Randolph, W.F. International drug scheduling. *Federal Register*, 1984, 49:29,273-29,274.

Rattray, M. Ecstasy: Toward an understanding of the biochemical basis of the actions of MDMA. *Essays in Biochemistry*, 1991, 26:77-87.

Reid, L.D., Hubbell, C.L., Tsai, J., and Fishkin, M.D. Naltrindole, a d-opioid antagonist, blocks MDMA's ability to enhance pressing for rewarding brain stimulation. *Pharmacology, Biochemistry, and Behavior*, 1996, 53:477-480.

Renfroe, C.L. MDMA on the street: Analysis anonymous. *Journal of Psychoactive Drugs*, 1986, 18:363-369.

Renton, R.J., Cowie, J.S., and Oon, M.C.H. A study of the precursors, intermediates and reaction by-products in the synthesis of 3,4-methylenedioxymethylamphetamine and its application to forensic drug analysis. *Forensic Science International*, 1993, 60:189-202.

Rezvani, A.H., Garges, P.L., Miller, D.B., and Gordon, C.J. Attenuation of alcohol consumption by MDMA (Ecstasy) in two strains of alcohol-preferring rats. *Pharmacology, Biochemistry and Behavior*, 1992, 43:103-110.

Ricaurte, G.A., Bryan, G., Strauss, L., Seiden, L., and Schuster, L. Hallucinogenic amphetamine selectively destroys brain serotonin nerve terminals. *Science*, 1985, 229:986-988.

Ricaurte, G.A., DeLanney, L.E., Irwin, I., and Langston, J.W. Toxic effects of MDMA on central serotonergic neurons in the primate: Importance of route and frequency of drug application. *Brain Research*, 1988, 446:165-169.

Ricaurte, G.A., DeLanney, L.E., Wiener, S.G., Irwin, I., and Langston, J.W. 5-Hydroxyindoleacetic acid in cerebrospinal fluid reflects serotonergic damage induced by 3,4-methylenedioxymethamphetamine in CNS of non-human primates. *Brain Research*, 1988, 474:359-363.

Ricaurte, G.A., Finnegan, K.T., Irwin, I., and Langston, J.W. Aminergic metabolites in cerebrospinal fluid of humans previously exposed to MDMA: Preliminary observations. *Annals of the New York Academy of Sciences*, 1990, 600:699-710.

Ricaurte, G.A., Forno, L.S., Wilson, M.A., DeLanney, L.E., Irwin, I., Molliver, M.E., and Langston, J.W. (+/-)-3,4-Methylenedioxymethamphetamine (MDMA) selectively damages central serotonergic neurons in nonhuman primates. *Journal of the American Medical Association*, 1988, 260:51-55.

Ricaurte, G.A., Marletto, A.L., Katz, J.L., and Marletto, M.B. Lasting effects of (+/-)-3,4-methylenedioxymethamphetamine (MDMA) on ventral serotonergic neurons in nonhuman primates: Neurochemical observations. *Journal of Pharmacology and Experimental Therapeutics*, 1992, 261:616-622.

Ricaurte, G.A., Markowska, A.L., Wenk, G.L., Hatzidimitriou, G., Wlos, J., and Olton, D.S. 3,4-Methylenedioxymethamphetamine, serotonin, and memory. *Journal of Pharmacology and Experimental Therapeutics*, 1993, 266:1097-2105.

Riedlinger, J.E. The scheduling of MDMA: A pharmacist's perspective. *Journal of Psychoactive Drugs*, 1985, 17:167-171.

Riedlinger, T. and Riedlinger, J. The "seven deadly sins" of media hype in light of the MDMA controversy. In T. Lyttle (Ed.), *Psychedelic Monographs and Essays*. Boynton Beach, FL: PM&E Publishing Group, 1989.

Rittoo, D.B. and Rittoo, D. Complications of "Ecstasy" misuse. *Lancet*, 1992, 340:725.

Rittoo, D., Rittoo, D.B., and Rittoo, D. Misuse of Ecstasy. *British Medical Journal*, 1992, 305:309-310.

Roberts, L. and Wright, H. Survival following intentional massive overdose of "Ecstasy." *Journal of Accident and Emergency Medicine,* 1993, 11:53-54.

Roberts, M. MDMA: Madness, not Ecstasy. *Psychology Today*, 20:14-15.

Roberts, T.B. Testimony on behalf of Drs. Grinspoon and Greer, Professors Bakalar and Roberts, United States Department of Justice, MDMA Administrative Law Hearings, 1985, Docket No. 84-48.

Robinson, T.E., Castaneda, E., and Whishaw, I.Q. Effects of cortical serotonin depletion induced by 3,4-methylenedioxymethamphetamine (MDMA) on behavior, before and after additional cholinergic blockade. *Neuropsychopharmacology*, 1993, 8:77-85.

Rohrig, T.P. and Prouty, R.W. Tissue distribution of methylenedioxymethamphetamine. *Journal of Analytical Toxicology,* 1992, 16:52-53.

Rosecrans, J.A. and Glennon, R.A. The effect of MDA and MDMA ("Ecstasy") isomers in combination with pirenpirone on operant responding in mice. *Pharmacology, Biochemistry, and Behavior,* 1987, 28:39-42.

Rosenbaum, M. and Doblin, R. Why MDMA should not have been made illegal. In Inciardi, J.A. (Ed.), *The Drug Legalization Debate.* Newbury Park, CA: Sage Publications, 1991.

Rosenbaum, M., Morgan, P., and Beck, J.E. Ethnographic notes on Ecstasy use among professionals. *International Journal of Drug Policy*, 1989, 1:16-19.

Rothwell, P.M. and Grant, R. Cerebral venous sinus thrombosis induced by "Ecstasy." *Journal of Neurology, Neurosurgery, and Psychiatry*, 1993, 56:1035.

Ruangyuttikan, W. and Moody, D.E. Comparison of three commercial amphetamine immunoassays for detection of methamphetamine, methylenedioxyamphetamine, methylenedioxymethamphetamine, and methylenedioxyethylamphetamine. *Journal of Analytical Toxicology*, 1988, 12:229-233.

Rudnick, G. and Wall, S.C. The molecular mechanism of "Ecstasy" [3,4-methylenedioxymethamphetamine(MDMA)]: Serotonin transporters are targets for MDMA-induced serotonin release. *Proceedings of the National Academy of Sciences of the United States of America*, 1992, 89:817-821.

Russell, B., Schwartz, R.H., and Dawling, S. Accidental ingestion of "Ecstasy" (3,4-methylenedioxymethamphetamine). *Archives of Disease in Childhood*, 1992, 67:1114-1115.

Rutty, G.N. and Milroy, C.M. The pathology of the ring-substituted amphetamine analogue 3,4-methylenedioxymethamphetamine (MDMA, "Ecstasy"). *Journal of Pathology*, 1997, 181:255-256.

Sabol, K.E., Lew, R., Richards, J.B., Vosmer, G.L., and Seiden, L.S. Methylenedioxymethamphetamine-induced serotonin deficits are followed by partial recovery over a 52-week period. Part I: Synaptosomal uptake and tissue concentration. *Journal of Pharmacology and Experimental Therapeutics*, 1996, 276:846-854.

Satchell, S.C. and Connaughton, M. Inappropriate antidiuretic hormone secretion and extreme rises in serum creatinine kinase following MDMA ingestion. *British Journal of Hospital Medicine*, 1994, 51:495.

Saunders, N. *E for Ecstasy.* London, England: Neal's Yard Desktop Publishing, 1993.

Saunders, N. Ecstasy and neurodegeneration. No evidence of neurotoxicity exists. *British Medical Journal*, 1996, 313:423.

Sawyer, J. and Stephens, W.P. Misuse of Ecstasy. *British Medical Journal*, 1992, 305:310.

Scallet, A.C., Lipe, G.W., Ali, S.F., Holson, R.R., Frith, C.H., and Slikker, W. Neuropathological evaluation by combined immunohistochemistry and degeneration-specific methods: Application to methylenedioxymethamphetamine. *Neurotoxicology*, 1988, 9:529-539.

Schechter, M.D. Discriminative profile of MDMA. *Pharmacology, Biochemistry, and Behavior*, 1986, 24:1533-1537.

Schechter, M.D. MDMA as a discriminative stimulus: Isomeric comparisons. *Pharmacology, Biochemistry, and Behavior*, 1987, 27:41-44.

Schechter, M.D. Serotonergic-dopaminergic mediation of 3,4-methylenedioxymethamphetamine (MDMA, "Ecstasy"). *Pharmacology, Biochemistry, and Behavior*, 1989, 31:817-824.

Schechter, M.D. Effect of MDMA neurotoxicity upon its conditioned place preference and discrimination. *Pharmacology, Biochemistry, and Behavior*, 1991, 38:539-544.

Schechter, M.D. Drug-drug discrimination: Stimulus properties of drugs of abuse upon a serotonergic-dopaminergic continuum. *Pharmacology, Biochemistry, and Behavior*, 1997, 56:89-96.

Scheffel, U., Lever, J.R., Stathis, M., and Ricaurte, G.A. Repeated administration of MDMA causes transient down-regulation of serotonin 5-HT-sub-2 receptors. *Neuropharmacology*, 1992, 31:881-893.

Scheffel, U. and Ricaurte, G.A. Paroxetine as an in vivo indicator of 3,4-methylenedioxymethamphetamine neurotoxicity: A presynaptic serotonergic positron emission tomography ligand. *Brain Research*, 1990, 527:89-95.

Schifano, F. Chronic atypical psychosis associated with MDMA ("Ecstasy") abuse. *Lancet,* 1991, 338:1335.

Schifano, F. and Magni, G. MDMA ("Ecstasy") abuse: Psychopathological features and craving for chocolate: A case series. *Biological Psychiatry,* 1994, 36:763-767.

Schmidt, C.J. Neurotoxicity of the psychedelic amphetamine, methylenedioxymethamphetamine. *Journal of Pharmacology and Experimental Therapeutics*, 1987, 240:1-7.

Schmidt, C.J., Abbate, G.M., Black, C.K., Taylor, V.L. Selective 5-hydroxytryptamine-2 receptor antagonists protect against the neurotoxicity of methylenedioxymethamphetamine in rats. *Journal of Pharmacology and Experimental Therapeutics*, 1990, 255:478-483.

Schmidt, C.J., Black, C.K., Abbate, G.M., and Taylor, V.L. Chloral hydrate anesthesia antagonizes the neurotoxicity of 3,4-methylenedioxymethamphetamine. *European Journal of Pharmacology*, 1990, 191:213-216.

Schmidt, C.J., Black, C.K., Abbate, G.M., and Taylor, V.L. Methylene-dioxymethamphetamine induced hyperthermia and neurotoxicity are independently mediated by 5-HT$_2$ receptors. *Brain Research*, 1990, 529:85-90.

Schmidt, C.J., Black, C.K., and Taylor, V.L. Antagonism of the neurotoxicity due to a single administration of methylenedioxymethamphetamine. *European Journal of Pharmacology*, 1990, 181:59-70.

Schmidt, C.J., Black, C.K., and Taylor, V.L. L-DOPA potentiation of the serotonergic deficits due to a single administration of 3,4-methylenedioxymethamphetamine, p-chloroamphetamine, or methamphetamine to rats. *European Journal of Pharmacology*, 1991, 203:41-49.

Schmidt, C.J., Fadayel, G.M., Sullivan, C.K., and Taylor, V.L. 5-HT$_2$ receptors exert a state-dependent regulation of dopaminergic function studies with MDL-100,907 and the amphetamine analogue, 3,4-methylenedioxymethamphetamine. *European Journal of Pharmacology*, 1992, 223:65-74.

Schmidt, C.J. and Kehne, J.H. Neurotoxicity of MDMA: Neurochemical effects. *Annals of the New York Academy of Science*, 1990, 600:665-681.

Schmidt, C.J., Levin, J.A., and Lovenberg, W. In vitro and in vivo neurochemical effects of methylenedioxymethamphetamine on striatal monoaminergic systems in the rat brain. *Biochemical Pharmacology*, 1987, 36:747-755.

Schmidt, C.J. and Taylor, V.L. Depression of rat brain tryptophan hydroxylase activity following the acute administration of methylenedioxymethamphetamine. *Biochemical Pharmacology*, 1987, 36:4095-4102.

Schmidt, C.J. and Taylor, V.L. Direct central effects of acute methylenedioxymethamphetamine on serotonergic neurons. *European Journal of Pharmacology*, 1988, 156:121-131.

Schmidt, C.J. and Taylor, V.L. Neurochemical effects of methylenedioxymethamphetamine in the rat: Acute versus long-term changes. In S.J. Peroutka (Ed.), *Ecstasy: The Clinical, Pharmacological, and Neurotoxicological Effects of the Drug MDMA*. Boston, MA: Kluwer Academic Publishers, 1990.

Schmidt, C.J. and Taylor, V.L. Reversal of the acute effect of 3,4-methylenedioxymethamphetamine by 5-HT uptake inhibitors. *European Journal of Pharmacology*, 1990, 181:133-136.

Schmidt, C.J., Taylor, V.L., Abbate, G.M., and Nieduzak, T.R. 5-HT$_2$ antagonist stereoselectively prevents the neurotoxicity of 3,4-methylenedioxymethamphetamine by blocking the acute stimulation of dopamine synthesis: Reversal by l-dopa. *Journal of Pharmacology and Experimental Therapeutics*, 1991, 256:230-235.

Schmidt, C.J., Wu, L., and Lovenberg, W. Methylenedioxymethamphetamine: A potentially neurotoxic amphetamine analogue. *European Journal of Pharmacology*, 1986, 124:175-178.

Screaton, G.R., Singer, M., Cairns, H.S., Thrasher, A., Sarner, M., and Cohen, S.L. Hyperpyrexia and rhabdomyolysis after MDMA ("Ecstasy") abuse. *Lancet*, 1992, 339:677-678.

Seiden, L.S. Testimony on behalf of the Drug Enforcement Administration, United States Department of Justice, MDMA Aministrative Law Hearings, 1985, Docket No. 84-48.

Seiden, L.S. and Sabol, K.E. Methamphetamine and methylenedioxymethamphetamine neurotoxicity: Possible mechanisms of cell destruction. *NIDA Research Monograph*, 1996, 163:251-276.

Series, H.G., Boeles, S., Dorkins, E., and Peveler, R. Psychiatric complications of "Ecstasy" use. *Journal of Psychopharmacology*, 1994, 8:60-61.

Series, H.G., Cowen, P.J., and Sharp, T. p-Chloroamphetamine (PCA), 3,4-methylenedioxymethamphetamine (MDMA) and d-fenfluramine pretreatment attenuates d-fenfluramine evoked release of 5-HT in vivo. *Psychopharmacology*, 1994, 116:508-514.

Series, H.G. and Lindefors, N. Ecstasy-Verkningar och toxicitet. *Lakartidningen*, 1993, 90:2648-2652.

Seymour, H.R., Gilman, D., and Quin, J.D. Severe ketoacidosis complicated by "Ecstasy" ingestion and exercise. *Diabetic Medicine*, 1996, 13:908-909.

Seymour, R. *MDMA*. San Francisco, CA: Haight Ashbury Publications, 1986.

Shannon, H.E. Testimony on behalf of the Drug Enforcement Administration, United States Department of Justice, MDMA Aministrative Law Hearings, 1985, Docket No. 84-48.

Sharkley, J., McBean, D.E., and Kelly, P.A. Alterations in hippocampal function following repeated exposure to the amphetamine derivative methylenedioxymethamphetamine ("Ecstasy"). *Psychopharmacology*, 1991, 105:113-118.

Shearman, J.D., Satsangi, J., Chapman, R.W.G., Ryley, N.G., and Weatherhead, S. Misuse of Ecstasy. *British Medical Journal*, 1992, 305:309.

Shulgin, A.T. Psychotomimetic drugs: Structure-activity relationships. In L.L. Iversen and S.H. Snyder (Eds.), *Handbook of Psychopharmacology*. New York: Plenum Press, 1978.

Shulgin, A.T. Twenty years on an ever-changing quest. In L. Grinspoon and J.B. Bakalar (Eds.), *Psychedelic Reflections*. New York: Human Science Press, 1983.

Shulgin, A.T. Personal letter to George Greer. Testimony submitted in the MDMA Administrative Law Hearings, 1985, Docket No. 84-48.

Shulgin, A.T. What is MDMA? *Pharmchem Newsletter*, 1985, 14:3-5,10-11.

Shulgin, A.T. The background and chemistry of MDMA. *Journal of Psychoactive Drugs*, 1986, 18:291-304.

Shulgin, A.T. History of MDMA. In S.J. Peroutka (Ed.), *Ecstasy: The Clinical, Pharmacological, and Neurotoxicological Effects of the Drug MDMA*. Boston, MA: Kluwer Academic Publishers, 1990.

Shulgin, A.T. How similar is substantially similar? *Journal of Forensic Sciences*, 1990, 35:8-10.

Shulgin, A.T. and Nichols, D.E. Characterization of three new psychotomimetics. In R.C. Stillman and R.E. Willette (Eds.), *The Psychopharmacology of Hallucinogens*. Elmsford, NY: Pergamon Press, 1978.

Siegel, R.K. Testimony on behalf of the Drug Enforcement Administration, United States Department of Justice, MDMA Aministrative Law Hearings, 1985, Docket No. 84-48.

Siegel, R.K. Chemical ecstasies. *Omni*, 1985, 8:29.

Siegel, R.K. MDMA: Nonmedical use and intoxication. *Journal of Psychoactive Drugs*, 1986, 18:349-354.

Simantov, R. and Tauber, M. The abused drug MDMA (Ecstasy) induces programmed death of human serotonergic cells. *FASEB*, 1997, 11:141-146.

Singarajah, C. and Lavies, N.G. An overdose of Ecstasy: A role for dantrolene. *Anaesthesia*, 1992, 47:686-687.

Slikker, W., Ali, S.F., Scallet, A.C., Firth, C.H., Newport, G.D., and Bailey, J.R. Neurochemical and neurohistological alterations in the rat and monkey produced by orally administered methylenedioxymethamphetamine (MDMA). *Toxicology and Applied Pharmacology*, 1988, 94:448-457.

Slikker, W., Holson, R.R., Ali, S.F., Kolta, M.G., Paule, M.G., Scallet, A.C., McMillan, D.E., Bailey, J.R., Hong, J.S., and Scalzo, F.M. Behavioral and neurochemical effects of orally administered MDMA in the rodent and nonhuman primate. *Neurotoxicology*, 1989, 10:529-542.

Smilkstein, M.J., Smolinske, S.C., and Rumack, B.H. A case of MAO inhibitor/ MDMA interaction: Agony after Ecstasy. *Clinical Toxicology*, 1987, 25:149-159.

Solowij, N. Ecstasy (3,4-methylenedioxymethamphetamine). *Current Opinion in Psychiatry*, 1993, 6:411-415.

Solowij, N., Hall, W., and Lee, N. Recreational MDMA use in Sydney: A profile of "Ecstasy" users and their experiences with the drug. *British Journal of Addictions*, 1992, 87:1161-1172.

Spanos, L.J. and Yamamoto, B.K. Acute and subchronic effects of methylenedioxymethamphetamine [(+/-)MDMA] on locomotion and serotonin syndrome behavior in the rat. *Pharmacology, Biochemistry, and Behavior.* 1989, 32:835-840.

Spatt, J., Glawar, B., and Mamoli, B. A pure amnestic syndrome after MDMA ("Ecstasy") ingestion. *Journal of Neurology, Neurosurgery, and Psychiatry*, 1997, 62:418-419.

Sprague, J.E., Huang, X., Kanthasamy, A., and Nichols, D.E. Attenuation of 3,4-methylenedioxymethamphetamine (MDMA) induced neurotoxicity with the serotonin precursors tryptophan and 5-hydroxytryptophan. *Life Sciences*, 1994, 55:1193-1198.

Sprague, J.E. and Nichols, D.E. Inhibition of MAO-B protects against MDMA-induced neurotoxicity in the striatum. *Psychopharmacology*, 1995, 118:357-359.

Sprague, J.E. and Nichols, D.E. The monoamine oxidase-B inhibitor L-deprenyl protects against 3,4-methylenedioxymethamphetamine lipid peroxidation and long-term serotonergic deficits. *Journal of Pharmacology and Experimental Therapeutics*, 1995, 273:667-673.

Sprouse, J.S., Bradberry, C.W., Roth, R.H., and Aghajanian, G.K. MDMA 3,4-methylenedioxymethamphetamine inhibits the firing of dorsal raphe neurons in brain slices via release of serotonin. *European Journal of Pharmacology*, 1989, 167:375-383.

Sprouse, J.S., Bradberry, C.W., Roth, R.H., and Aghajanian, G.K. 3,4-Methylenedioxymethamphetamine-induced release of serotonin and inhibition of dorsal raphe cell firing: Potentiation by L-tryptophane. *European Journal of Pharmacology*, 1990, 178:313-320.

Squier, M.V., Jalloh, S., Jones-Hilton, D., and Series, H. Death after Ecstasy ingestion: Neuropathological findings. *Journal of Neurology, Neurosurgery, and Psychiatry*, 1995, 58:756-764.

Sreenivasan, V.R. Problems in identification of methylenedioxy and methoxy amphetamines. *The Journal of Criminal Law, Criminology, and Police Science*, 1972, 63:304-312.

Steele, T.D., Brewster, W.K., Johnson, M.P., Nichols, D.E., and Yim, G.K.W. Assessment of the role of alpha-methylepinine in the neurotoxicity of MDMA. *Pharmacology, Biochemistry, and Behavior*, 1991, 38:345-351.

Steele, T.D., McCann, U.D., and Ricaurte, G.A. 3,4-Methylenedioxymethamphetamine (MDMA, "Ecstasy"): Pharmacology and toxicology in animals and humans. *Addiction*, 1994, 89:539-551.

Steele, T.D., Nichols, D.E., and Yim, G.K.W. Stereochemical effects of 3,4-methylenedioxymethamphetamine (MDMA) and related amphetamine derivatives on inhibition of uptake of [^{3}H]-monoamines into synaptosomes from different regions of rat brain. *Biochemical Pharmacology*, 1987, 36:2297-2303.

Steele, T.D., Nichols, D.E., and Yim, G.K.W. 3,4-Methylenedioxymethamphetamine transiently alters mouse brain and cardiac biogenic amines. *Pharmacology, Biochemistry, and Behavior*, 1989, 34:223-227.

Stone, D.M., Hanson, G.R., and Gibb, J.W. Differences in the central serotonergic effects of methylenedioxymethamphetamine (MDMA) in mice and rats. *Neuropharmacology*, 1987, 26:1657-1661.

Stone, D.M., Johnson, M., Hanson, G.R., and Gibb, J.W. A comparison of the neurotoxic potential of methylenedioxyamphetamine (MDA) and its N-methylated and N-ethylated derivatives. *European Journal of Pharmacology*, 1987, 134:245-248.

Stone, D.M., Johnson, M., Hanson, G.R., and Gibb, J.W. Role of endogenous dopamine in the central serotonergic deficits induced by 3,4-methylenedioxymethamphetamine. *Journal of Pharmacology and Experimental Therapeutics*, 1988, 247:79-87.

Stone, D.M., Johnson, M., Hanson, G.R., and Gibb, J.W. Acute inactivation of tryptophan hydroxylase by amphetamine analogs involves the oxidation of sulfhydryl sites. *European Journal of Pharmacology*, 1989, 172:93-97.

Stone, D.M., Merchant, K.M., Hanson, G.R., and Gibb, J.W. Immediate and long-term effects of 3,4-methylenedioxymethamphetamine on serotonin pathways in brain of rat. *Neuropharmacology*, 1987, 26:1677-1683.

Stone, D.M., Stahl, D.C., Hanson, G.R., and Gibb, J.W. The effects of 3,4-methylenedioxymethamphetamine (MDMA) and 3,4-methylenedioxyamphetamine (MDA) on monoaminergic systems in the rat brain. *European Journal of Pharmacology*, 1986, 128:41-48.

St. Omer, V.E., Ali, S.F., Holson, R.R., Duhart, H.M., Scalzo, F.M., and Slikker, W. Behavioral and neurochemical effects of prenatal methylenedioxymethamphetamine (MDMA) exposure in rats. *Neurotoxicology and Teratology*, 1991, 13:13-20.

Strassman, R.J. Testimony on behalf of Drs. Grinspoon and Greer, Professors Bakalar and Roberts, United States Department of Justice, MDMA Administrative Law Hearings, 1985, Docket No. 84-48.

Suarez, R.V. and Riemersma, R. "Ecstasy" and sudden cardiac death. *The American Journal of Forensic Medicine and Pathology*, 1988, 9:339-341.

Szukaj, M. MDMA ("Ecstasy")—A dangerous drug or psychotherapeutic drug? *Nervenarzt*, 1994, 65:802-805.

Taraska, T. and Finnegan, K.T. Nitric oxide and the neurotoxic effects of methamphetamine and 3,4-methylenedioxymethamphetamine. *Journal of Pharmacology and Experimental Therapeutics*, 1997, 280:941-947.

Taylor, M. Catatonia: A review of the behavioral neurological syndrome. *Neuropsychiatry, Neuropsychology, and Behavioral Neurology*, 1990, 3:48-72.

Teggin, A.F. Ecstasy—A dangerous drug. *South African Medical Journal*, 1992, 87:431-432.

Thomasius, R., Schmolke, M., and Kraus, D. MDMA ("Ecstasy") use: An overview of psychiatric and medical sequelae. *Fortschritte der Neurologie—Psychiatrie*, 1997, 65:49-61.

Thompson, D.M., Winsauer, P.J., and Mastropaolo, J. Effects of phencyclidine, ketamine, and MDMA on complex operant behavior in monkeys. *Pharmacology, Biochemistry, and Behavior*, 1987, 26:401-405.

Tocus, E.C. Testimony on behalf of the Drug Enforcement Administration, United States Department of Justice, MDMA Aministrative Law Hearings, 1985, Docket No. 84-48.

Toufexis, A. A crackdown on Ecstasy. *Time*, 1985, 125:64.

Tucker, G.T., Lennard, M.S., Ellis, S.W., Woods, H.F., Cho, A.K., Lin, L.Y., Hiratsuka, A., Schmitz, D.A., and Chu, T.Y. The demethylenation of methylenedioxymethamphetamine ("Ecstasy") by debrisoquine hydroxylase (CYP2D6). *Biochemical Pharmacology*, 1994, 47:151-156.

Tyler, A. *Street Drugs*. London, England: Hodder and Stoughton, 1995.

Verebey, K., Alrazi, J., and Jaffe, J.H. The complications of "Ecstasy" (MDMA). *Journal of the American Medical Association*, 1988, 259:649-650.

Verweij, A.M. Clandestine manufacture of 3,4-methylenedioxymethamphetamine (MDMA) by low pressure reductive amination. A mass spectrometric study of some reaction mixtures. *Forensic Science International*, 1990, 45:91-96.

Verweij, A.M. Mass-spectrometry data of some metabolites of the amphetamine derivatives 3,4-methylenedioxyamphetamine (MDA) and 3,4-methylenedioxymethamphetamine (MDMA). *Archiv fur Kriminologie*, 1996, 197:27-30.

von Wilmsdorff, M. and Gastpar, M. Brain functional disorders after taking Ecstasy. *Deutsche Medizinische Wochenschrift*, 1995, 120:1716.

Wake, D. Ecstasy overdose: A case study. *Intensive and Critical Care Nursing*, 1995, 11:6-9.

Walsh, T., Carmichael, R., and Chestnut, J. A hyperthermic reaction to "Ecstasy." *British Journal of Hospital Medicine*, 1994, 51:476.

Wang, S.S., Ricaurte, G.A., and Peroutka, S.J. [^{3}H]3,4-methylenedioxymethamphetamine (MDMA) interactions with brain membranes and glass fiber filter paper. *European Journal of Pharmacology*, 1987, 138:439-443.

Watson, L. and Beck, J. New age seekers: MDMA use as an adjunct to spiritual pursuit. *Journal of Psychoactive Drugs*, 1991, 23:261-270.

Webb, C. and Williams, V. Ecstasy intoxification: Appreciation of complications and the role of dantrolene. *Anaesthesia*, 1993, 48:542-543.

Weil, A. and Rosen, W. *From Chocolate to Morphine*. Boston, MA: Houghton Mifflin, 1993.

Whitaker-Azmitia, P.M. and Aronson, T.A. "Ecstasy" (MDMA)-induced panic. *American Journal of Psychiatry*, 1989, 146:119.

Whitaker-Azmitia, P.M. and Azmitia, E.C. A tissue culture model of MDMA toxicity. In S.J. Peroutka (Ed.), *Ecstasy: The Clinical, Pharmacological, and Neurotoxicological Effects of the Drug MDMA*. Boston, MA: Kluwer Academic Publishers, 1990.

White, J.M., Bochner, F., and Irvine, R.J. The agony of "Ecstasy." *Medical Journal of Australia*, 1997, 166:117-118.

White, S.R., Duffy, P., and Kalivas, P.W. Methylenedioxymethamphetamine depresses glutamate evoked neuronal firing and increases extracellular levels of dopamine and serotonin in the nucleus accumbens in vivo. *Neuroscience*, 1994, 62:41-50.

White, S.R., Obradovic, T., Imel, K.M., and Wheaton, M.J. The effects of methylenedioxymethamphetamine (MDMA, "Ecstasy") on monoaminergic neurotransmission in the central nervous system. *Progress in Neurobiology*, 1996, 49:455-479.

Wichems, C.H., Hollingsworth, C.K., and Bennett, B.A. Release of serotonin induced by 3,4-methylenedioxymethamphetamine (MDMA) and other substituted amphetamines in cultured fetal raphe neurons: Further evidence for calcium-independent mechanisms of release. *Brain Research*, 1995, 695:10-18.

Wilkerson, G. and London, E.D. Effects of methylenedioxymethamphetamine on local cerebral glucose utilization in the rat. *Neuropharmacology*, 1989, 28:1129-1138.

Wilkins, B. Hyponatraemia must be treated with low water input. *British Medical Journal*, 1996, 313:689-690.

Williams, H., Meagher, D., and Galligan, P. MDMA ("Ecstasy"): A case of possible drug-induced psychosis. *Irish Journal of Medical Science*, 1993, 34:43-44.

Williams, A. and Unwin, R. Prolonged elevation of serum creatine kinase (CK) without renal failure after ingestion of Ecstasy. *Nephrology, Dialysis, Transplantation*, 1997, 12:361-362.

Wilson, M.A., Ricaurte, G.A., and Molliver, M.E. Distinct morphologic classes of serotonergic axons in primates exhibit differential vulnerability to the psychotropic drug 3,4-methylenedioxymethamphetamine. *Neuroscience*, 1989, 28:121-137.

Winslow, J.T. and Insel, T.R. Serotonergic modulation of rat pup ultrasonic vocal development: Studies with 3,4-methylenedioxymethamphetamine. *Journal of Pharmacology and Experimental Therapeutics*, 1990, 254:212-220.

Winstock, A.R. Chronic paranoid psychosis after misuse of MDMA. *British Medical Journal*, 1991, 302:1150-1151.

Wodarz, N. and Boning, J. "Ecstasy"-induced psychotic depersonalization syndrome. *Nevenarzt*, 1993, 64:478-480.

Wolff, K., Hay, A.W.M., Sherlock, K., and Conner, M. Contents of "Ecstasy." *Lancet*, 1995, 346:1100-1101.

Wolfson, P.E. Testimony on behalf of Drs. Grinspoon and Greer, Professors Bakalar and Roberts, United States Department of Justice, MDMA Administrative Law Hearings, 1985, Docket No. 84-48.

Wolfson, P.E. Meetings at the edge with Adam (Ecstasy): A man for all seasons. *Journal of Psychoactive Drugs*, 1986, 18:329-333.

Wotherspoon, G., Savery, D., Priestly, J.V., and Rattray, M. Repeated administration of MDMA down-regulates pre-procholecystokinin mRNA expression but not tyrosine hydroxylase mRNA expression in neurons of the rat substantia nigra. *Molecular Brain Research*, 1994, 25:34-40.

Yamamoto, B.K., Nash, J.F., and Gudelsky, G.A. Modulation of methylenedioxymethamphetamine induced striatal dopamine release by the interaction between serotonin and gamma-aminobutyric acid in the substantia nigra. *Journal of Pharmacology and Experimental Therapeutics*, 1995, 273:1063-1070.

Yamamoto, B.K. and Spanos, L.J. The acute effects of methylenedioxymethamphetamine on dopamine release in the awake behaving rat. *European Journal of Pharmacology*, 1988, 148:195-204.

Yau, J.L., Kelly, P.A., Sharkey, J., and Seckijr, J.R. Chronic 3,4-methylenedioxymethamphetamine administration decreases glucocorticoid and mineralocorticoid receptor, but increases 5-hydroxytryptamine-1C receptor gene expression in the rat hippocampus. *Neuroscience*, 1994, 61:31-40.

Yeh, SY. Lack of protective effect of chloropromazine on 3,4-methylenedioxymethamphetamine induced neurotoxicity on brain serotonin neurons in rats. *Research Communications in Substance Abuse*, 1990, 11:167-174.

Yeh, S.Y. and Hsu, F.L. The neurochemical and stimulatory effects of putative metabolites of 3,4-methylenedioxyamphetamine and 3,4-methylenedioxymethamphetamine in rats. *Pharmacology, Biochemistry, and Behavior*, 1991, 39:787-790.

Yensen, R. Testimony on behalf of Drs. Grinspoon and Greer, Professors Bakalar and Roberts, United States Department of Justice, MDMA Administrative Law Hearings, 1985, Docket No. 84-48.

Young, F.L. MDMA Administrative Law Hearings; United States Department of Justice, Drug Enforcement Administration, Prehearing Conference, 1985, Docket No. 84-48.

Young, F.L. MDMA Administrative Law Hearings; United States Department of Justice, Drug Enforcement Administration. Opinion and recommended ruling, findings of fact, conclusions of law, and decision of Administrative Law Judge, 1986, Docket No. 84-48.

Yousif, M.Y., Fitzgerald, R.L., Narasimhachari, N., Rosecrans, J.A., Blanke, R.V., and Glennon, R.A. Identification of metabolites of 3,4-methylenedioxyme-thamphetamine in rats. *Drug and Alcohol Dependence*, 1990, 26:127-135.

Zacny, J.P., Virus, R.M., and Woolverton, W.L. Tolerance and cross-tolerance to 3,4-methylenedioxymethamphetamine, methamphetamine and methylenedioxy-amphetamine. *Pharmacology, Biochemistry, and Behavior*, 1990, 35:637-642.

Zinberg, N. *Drugs, Set, and Setting*. New Haven, CT: Yale University Press, 1984.

Index

Page numbers followed by the letter "t" indicate tables; those followed by the letter "f" indicate figures.

Order Your Own Copy of
This Important Book for Your Personal Library!

THE LOVE DRUG
Marching to the Beat of Ecstasy

_____ in hardbound at $39.95 (ISBN: 0-7890-0453-4)

_____ in softbound at $17.95 (ISBN: 0-7890-0454-2)

COST OF BOOKS_____	☐ **BILL ME LATER:** ($5 service charge will be added)
	(Bill-me option is good on US/Canada/Mexico orders only;
OUTSIDE USA/CANADA/	not good to jobbers, wholesalers, or subscription agencies.)
MEXICO: ADD 20%_____	
	☐ Check here if billing address is different from
POSTAGE & HANDLING_____	shipping address and attach purchase order and
(US: $3.00 for first book & $1.25	billing address information.
for each additional book)	
Outside US: $4.75 for first book	
& $1.75 for each additional book)	Signature_____
SUBTOTAL_____	☐ **PAYMENT ENCLOSED: $**_____
IN CANADA: ADD 7% GST_____	☐ **PLEASE CHARGE TO MY CREDIT CARD.**
STATE TAX_____	☐ Visa ☐ MasterCard ☐ AmEx ☐ Discover
(NY, OH & MN residents, please	
add appropriate local sales tax)	Account # _____
FINAL TOTAL_____	Exp. Date _____
(If paying in Canadian funds,	
convert using the current	Signature _____
exchange rate. UNESCO	
coupons welcome.)	

Prices in US dollars and subject to change without notice.

NAME _____

INSTITUTION _____

ADDRESS _____

CITY _____

STATE/ZIP _____

COUNTRY _____ COUNTY (NY residents only) _____

TEL _____ FAX _____

E-MAIL_____

May we use your e-mail address for confirmations and other types of information? ☐ Yes ☐ No

Order From Your Local Bookstore or Directly From
The Haworth Press, Inc.
10 Alice Street, Binghamton, New York 13904-1580 • USA
TELEPHONE: 1-800-HAWORTH (1-800-429-6784) / Outside US/Canada: (607) 722-5857
FAX: 1-800-895-0582 / Outside US/Canada: (607) 772-6362
E-mail: getinfo@haworthpressinc.com
PLEASE PHOTOCOPY THIS FORM FOR YOUR PERSONAL USE.

BOF96